11937

14.00

D0352939

The Essential Guide for
Competent Teaching
Assistants

The Essential Guide for

Competent Teaching Assistants

Meeting the National Occupational Standards at Level 2

ANNE WATKINSON

with contributions by
Margaret Bickmore and Ian Roper

David Fulton Publishers

London

David Fulton Publishers Ltd
The Chiswick Centre, 414 Chiswick High Road, London W4 5TF
www.fultonpublishers.co.uk

David Fulton Publishers is a division of Granada Learning, part of the Granada
Media group.

First published 2003
10 9 8 7 6 5 4 3 2

British Library Cataloguing in Publication Data
A catalogue record for this book is available from the British Library.

ISBN 1 84312 008 9

Typeset by Servis Filmsetting Ltd, Manchester
Printed and bound by The Thanet Press, Margate.

Contents

Preface

This book aims to provide the underpinning knowledge to support teaching assistants (TAs) in all phases of schooling when undertaking study at a basic level. It assumes that you, the TA, are already working in a school, possibly in a voluntary capacity, but wish to learn more about the job you are doing and may be considering undertaking some formal course for TAs locally. It contains practical examples of TAs at work, and ideas for you to try out. In actively learning about the work you do, you will gain in confidence and understanding of the purpose of the tasks you are asked to undertake. In assuming that you are wanting to try out some of the ideas in your school, it is important that you talk over any practical issues with someone in authority in the school. This may be your line manager if you have one, or the class teacher with whom you are most closely associated. If you are unsure about these people, approach the person who appointed you, a senior manager or in a primary school the head teacher. The school may then appoint someone to be your mentor, so that you can discuss any issues that arise as you read or use the book.

Involving you, the reader, in your own learning will help you understand how pupils learn, how to develop skills to support the teacher and various aspects of the curriculum. It firmly embeds practice of the TA within a whole-school context, enabling you to understand your role in supporting the school, and taking appropriate responsibility for aspects of care, health, safety and well-being of pupils with whom you come into contact, and to play your full part in the school team. These practical ways of accessing the knowledge you need to understand why teachers do what they do, will enable you to support more fully their instructions. This knowledge will give you confidence to use your initiative and experience appropriately, to support teachers usefully, to help pupils learn and access the curriculum. In promoting active learning with the school's support, it will enable you to become part of the learning community of the school, fulfilling the school policies and participating in the formation of the whole-school ethos.

The book can be used to support National Vocational Qualifications (NVQs) or other TA awards at Level 2 and is related to the competencies described in the National Occupational Standards (NOS) at Level 2. These are referred to in the text (for example, [2–5.1: ii & vi]) and can be found in full by accessing the web site of the publishers, the Local Government National Training Organisation (LGNTO) (www.lgnto.gov.uk).

Acknowledgements

I would like to thank:

- Margaret Bickmore and Ian Roper, both Curriculum Development Advisers for Essex County Council Learning Services, for their contribution of the whole of Chapter 9. I could not have written the book without them;
- John Acklaw, a Chartered Educational Psychologist, for his suggestions and help with Chapter 6;
- Essex County Council Learning Services for their permission to reproduce their format for an Individual Education Plan; and the Employer's Organisation for local government (formerly the Local Government National Training Organisation) for permission to reproduce the Values and Principles Underpinning the National Occupational Standards for Teaching/ Classroom Assistants;
- Beehive Lane Community Primary School, Chelmsford, Essex; Maldon Primary School, Essex; Our Lady of Peace Junior School, Slough and its ex-head teacher Geraldine Lindley; as well as Stewards School, Harlow, Essex for permission to use examples of their documentation;
- Mary Mills, SENCO of Maldon Primary School; Terry O'Neill, Assistant Head of Stewards School; and Frank Bonner, Staff Development Manager of Kingsdown School, Southend, for their time, help and suggestions;
- the many schools and TAs, whose practice and friendship has been a constant inspiration throughout my work with them;
- Margaret Haigh of David Fulton Publishers for her encouragement and help while preparing the book;
- my husband Frank, for his endless patience, domestic help and support with my ICT systems.

List of abbreviations

ABC	Awarding Body Consortium
AE	Adult education
ALS	Additional Literacy Support
BTEC	Business and Technology Education Council
CACHE	Council for Awards in Children's Care and Education
CPD	Continous professional development
DfEE	Department for Education and Employment
DfES	Department for Education and Skills
DML	Daily mathematics lesson
DOH	Department of Health
DT	Design and technology
EAL	English as an additional language
ELS	Early Literacy Support
EO	Employers Organisation
FE	Further education
GCSE	General Certificate of Secondary Education
HE	Higher education
HMI	Her Majesty's Inspectorate
HO	Home Office
ICT	Information and communication technology
IEP	Individual education plan
IiP	Investors in People
INSET	In-service education for teachers
LEA	Local education authority
LGNTO	Local Government National Training Organisation
LMS	Local Management of Schools
LSA	Learning support assistant
NC	National Curriculum
NCFE	Northern College of Further Education
NJC	National Joint Council for Local Government Services
NLNS	National Literacy and Numeracy Strategies
NLS	National Literacy Strategy
NNS	National Numeracy Strategy
NOCN	National Open College Network

NOS	National Occupational Standards
NVQ	National Vocational Qualification
OCR	Oxford and Cambridge and RSA Examinations
Ofsted	Office for Standards in Education
OHP	Overhead projector
OMS	Oral and mental starter
OU	Open University
PE	Physical education
PGCE	Postgraduate Certificate of Education
PIPS	Progression in phonics
PSHE	Personal, social and health education
QCA	Qualifications and Curriculum Authority
QTS	Qualified Teacher Status
RSA	Royal Society of Arts
SDP	School development plan
SEN	Special educational needs
SENCO	Special educational needs coordinator
SIP	School improvement plan
STAC	Specialist Teacher Assistant Certificate
TA	Teaching assistant
VAK	Visual, auditory and kinaesthetic

1 Introduction

The reason for this book

Teaching assistants (TAs) are big news. Over the last five years, their importance has been recognised. There are few schools that do not have them, although they may call them by different titles and utilise them in different ways. The government has put considerable resources into the recruitment, training and support of systems for professional and career development, including facilitating pathways to teaching for those who wish it. One of the ways in which TAs received national recognition was by the commissioning of National Occupational Standards (NOS), now available for most employees in recognised jobs. For TAs, these were first published in the summer of 2001 after considerable consultation by the firm contracted with the task, Miller West Ltd (LGNTO 2001).

This was no easy matter. The role of TAs is complex and varied, as well as their name. Every reader of this book probably does something different from his or her colleagues, even within the same school. The first job within the consultation was to draw up a function map based on known similar jobs. There were already NOS for those working in the early years, science technicians and those working in the care sectors, but not for those working in schools for pupils of compulsory school age or older. Existing job descriptions focused on the role of the TA in supporting teachers: the sort of ancillary, paintpot washing, domestic task role; supporting pupils: a result of the emphasis on supporting those with special educational needs (SEN) within the system; and supporting the school: the photocopying, making the tea, accompanying visits and making costumes sort of role. However, during the latter part of the 1990s, the National Literacy and Numeracy Strategies (NLNS) brought the work of TAs into the limelight, with the emphasis on group work, and the provision of highly structured resources which TAs could use to support the strategies. This means TAs have become familiar with curriculum content. Primary schools have become more focused on the subjects of the curriculum and the public, especially parents, have become concerned about the results being achieved in various subjects in primary and secondary schools through the publication of league tables. Thus, these four strands of support became the first stage in the TA function map.

However, all of you will immediately see that whatever you do often involves at least two strands of these four if not all of them. Any support for a pupil in class means understanding the curriculum objective of the teacher, following the policy for that subject given by the school, working in partnership with the teacher of that class as well as being with that pupil. Writing standards to describe this TA role was no easy matter, and the units, when finally composed, could not follow that neat four-strand pattern. This book is largely based round these four strands as it has got to have some sort of organisation, and while there will always be the constant perception that the role is a multi-dimensional one, it seemed a helpful way to proceed. It could have followed the units of the national standards, but they may change with reviews, they may not be relevant to all TAs in terms of following a full NVQ procedure, and other awards for TAs may appear which do not follow the pattern of the NOS. This book is an attempt to lay foundations for TAs, whatever your professional development needs.

Having supported TAs through various courses, awards and professional development programmes in the past, I found there was little reading matter for them apart from materials produced for teachers, and books largely for those supporting pupils with SEN or in the early years sector. Being a TA is largely a practical job, but there is a need for you to know and understand what you are doing, to underpin your practice. Some of this can only come from consulting the teachers responsible for setting your tasks, and understanding why you are asked to do a task makes the task more interesting and more effective. Time and again on courses, TAs say, 'Now I know why I was asked to do that.' But, being a practical job, just reading a book about the job will not be enough; practice and theory must go together, hence the need to work with the existing staff at your school and not in isolation. With the practice linked to knowledge and understanding of your job, you will gain confidence and become more effective. This in turn makes the teachers' job easier, helps the pupils learn more effectively and enjoyably, gives you more job satisfaction and supports the purposes of the school.

Who the book is for

The book is intended for those of you who have recently started in the job, or who are working as volunteers and are keen to understand more about the role. The NOS Level 2 define what a competent TA should be able to do, but 'whose responsibilities are limited in scope' (LGNTO 2001, Level 2, p. 2). If you read all this book, do many of the activities, and enrol for a Level 2 course at a local study centre, you will be in a good position to get a Level 2 award, showing your competence to be a good TA. This award would prove to any prospective employer that you know what you are doing, know what the job entails whether you are working in the primary or secondary sector, or a middle school system, whether you are to support a named pupil or carry out a specific curriculum programme. If you are working in a special school, it is likely that you may need some specialist training in addition to such a course, as the pupils you work with will have particular special needs. For you, undertaking such a study in the generalist areas of school work will stand you in good stead should your job change, or you want to enter mainstream schools or to know more about the general ways in which education works.

Only you can learn about your job. Knowledge and understanding cannot be fed to you without you digesting it, taking it in and using it. You must take personal responsibility for your continuing professional development. You may want to show off your acquisition by undertaking assignments for others to read or even enter them into some kind of awards system, but fundamentally, all adults are still learners, and responsible for their own learning and progress. If you have not studied since leaving school, you may need to consider your own study skills to help you adjust, but dipping into some of the ideas in this book will help you on your way.

How this book can be used

This book can be read and acted on in the sequence in which it is written, which may take some time if all the activities are carried out, but even then it is not intended to be a course on its own. Not only should you make sure that someone in the school is aware that you want to better yourself, increase your knowledge and understanding of the way in which you can support teaching and learning, but also sharing your ideas and thoughts on the content with others is important. If you wish to undertake work towards awards then seek out a local provider, preferably with the guidance and possibly even with the financial support of your school, and register for an accredited award. This book can then be your back-up text. If you undertake an award you will find that you do not have to cover all the content of this book to gain the award but you may find the bits you are not covering for the award are still relevant to the job you are doing.

The real intention of the book is that it can be a reference book, not worked through tediously page by page but just a few relevant pages used at a time. Use the index to find what you need, read that bit, do any associated activities and make any notes for your own future reference. Discuss the reading with others in the school or on your course and remember anything you feel is important to use in your daily work. Not everything you will want to know will be found in this book – few books can ever provide such reference – but it will give references to other specialist texts, most of which should either be in your school resource collection or one of the teachers may have it at home. Chapter 2 starts from yourself, gives you ideas on ways in which you can help yourself to learn and undertake professional and personal development and some practical ways to proceed. Start by reading Chapter 2 to help you set yourself in the context of your job and your school, and begin a way of recording your thoughts and information. Then progress to the chapter or section that you feel most relates to your needs.

However, you do not work in isolation. It is essential that all that you do in school fits in with the way things are done in that school, and that you play your part as a member of staff, whether or not you are paid to work in the school. Chapter 3 explores the importance of relationships and how this underpins work in any area or organisation. It gives you some understanding of the people involved in a school. Chapter 4 deals with all the issues about working in a school that you will have to take note of, gives the school context of which you must become aware, and explores the structures, systems and procedures that go to make up a school which you will support. Chapters 5 to 10 then cover the other three strands of support mentioned above, starting with the pupils and their learning, then focusing on supporting the teacher and teaching, and the curriculum, where there are separate sections, some contributed by experts in their subjects showing how you can support the curriculum objectives while working with pupils under the direction of the teachers.

Some of the chapters are subdivided. The activities for you to try are in framed boxes. These can be photocopied to work on separately and changed to suit your circumstances if you wish. Try out some of these exercises to give you examples of things mentioned in the text you are reading and this will help you internalise the meaning. In addition, in each chapter you will find mini case studies. Some of these are fictional, but all of them are based on good practice that I have seen in the many schools I have worked in or visited. Even where the stories are factual, all the names have been changed to preserve the participants' anonymity. After you have tried out the ideas for yourself, you will begin to recognise examples of good practice for yourself within your own school, and may be able to write a few scenarios of your own. You can see that to get the best from the book it is important to do it with someone experienced in the ways of your school to share your ideas and feelings with – the need for an in-school mentor. It could be that you find examples of ways of working that puzzle you or are quite different from those described here. It is then vital that you have someone with whom you can discuss the matters, to find out why things are done in that way in your school. There will be a good reason for the differences, which will provide yet another learning point for you. All schools are different, even if they are in the same area, of the same size and age, and take in similar aged children. People make them different, just as homes in a row of similar houses are all different.

The National Occupational Standards

The standards for TAs were consulted on and tried out over a period of well over a year before they were published. Both experts in the field of education and practitioners commented on them. They were designed 'to be suitable for all staff in England, Scotland, Wales and Northern Ireland who work with teachers in classrooms supporting the learning process in primary, special and secondary schools' (LGNTO 2001, Introduction, p. 2). Teaching/classroom assistant was the generic title used to cover all the variety of names used by schools. The term preferred by the DfES (DfEE 2000a) is teaching assistant, but Scotland, having its own education system, preferred classroom assistant, hence the dual nomenclature in the standards. The shortened form TA will be used in this book as many references will be to Acts of Parliament and codes of practice which are sometimes changed for use in the principalities other than England. Some differences in the four countries are noted in the text, for instance in referring to the requirements of the National Curriculum (NC).

'National Occupational Standards are descriptors of best practice for a particular function' (LGNTO 2001, Introduction, p. 3). However, because they follow a pattern set out for all occupations, the format and language used are often unfamiliar to the newcomer. Because they are vocationally based they set out to define competence – what the person fulfilling that role 'can do'. Sometimes they are referred to as 'can do' statements. But no job is just about doing; for all of them some kind of underpinning knowledge and understanding is required, so the standards give statements both about performance – 'performance indicators' – and knowledge.

In order to allow for different levels of competence and understanding, NOS are given in different levels. Level 1 defines the kind of job that is routine and repetitive such as may be found on a factory floor. It is quickly recognised that when one is dealing with people rather than things, and especially when dealing with children or young people, nothing is ever repetitive. In fact one of the joys of working in a school is that no two days are ever the same. So there is no Level 1 in educational standards. Level 2 is seen as the basic level and is roughly equivalent to higher GCSE or O level grades in its knowledge requirements. Level 3 is the more advanced level, for those working across a range of responsibilities within an institution; study for an NVQ at Level 3 equates to that of A levels. Level 4, which does not yet exist as NOS for teaching/classroom assistants, would be equivalent to a degree or management level. Some of the TA courses found in higher education (HE) institutions, such as the Open University Specialist Teacher Assistant Certificate (OU STAC) course, and the new foundation degrees are at degree study level. Qualified Teacher Status (QTS) implies not only graduate status, but also the professional qualifications needed by a teacher. Some degrees in teacher training institutions lead to the acquisition of both, and some require the recipient to take a further year's study to obtain a Postgraduate Certificate of Education (PGCE). All newly qualified teachers have to undergo a period of at least one year's induction, which is monitored before they are fully accredited as qualified teachers. In the last chapter of the book the current status of qualifications and potential routes to teaching for the 10–15 per cent of TAs who might wish to take that route are expanded.

Most of you just want to be a good TA. For you, the NOS set the standards you should be aiming to attain. TAs who currently have been in post since before their publication will already have considerable experience 'under their belts'. For them, the book giving the underpinning knowledge for Level 3, *Becoming an experienced teaching assistant*, would be more appropriate. A new high level TA status is now being proposed (DfES 2002a), and more information will be available about this in 2003.

The levels are divided into units, some of which are considered essential for any TA in any kind of school. If taking an NVQ, these units would be considered 'mandatory'. Each level also contains some optional units, but this book will cover all the possible units for Level 2, as it is impossible to determine who would want information on which units. At Level 2, obtaining the NVQ would require showing evidence for the four mandatory units and three of the five optional units detailed below.

Mandatory units
    2-1: Help with classroom resources and records
    2-2: Help with the care and support of pupils
    2-3: Provide support for learning activities
    2-4: Provide effective support for your colleagues

Optional units
    2-5: Support literacy and numeracy activities in the classroom
    3-1: Contribute to the management of pupil behaviour
    3-10: Support the maintenance of pupil safety and security
    3-11: Contribute to the heath and well-being of pupils
    3-17: Support the use of ICT in the classroom

Each unit has at least two elements, the standards themselves. These are sections covering different aspects of that part of the TA role. The unit also includes a glossary of terms for the unit and a brief summary description of who the unit is for, what it is about, what it contains and what you would need to show in order to prove your competence in that area of your work. Each standard is then subdivided into 'performance indicators', 'knowledge base' and the 'scope' that would be required of a person performing to that level. Each of these subsections may have many (three or four to 13 or so) sentences defining the subsection. In other words, the NOS are very detailed, covering 42 pages for Level 2 and 111 pages for Level 3. Hence they are not reproduced in this book, you must get hold of a separate copy for yourself from the LGNTO website (www.lgnto.gov.uk). The NOS standard titles are given in Table 1.1 along with some indication of where you might find material in this book to support the contents.

You do need to get a copy of the standards, for at the beginning of each unit there is a helpful description of what is involved in your work in the area. While this book does not follow the structure of the NOS, it does contain cross-references to all the units and elements mentioned by them. The relevant NOS references are given in square brackets in the text. Hopefully, should you need them for a course or for your portfolio (see Chapter 2 for details of this way of keeping your work together), this book will ease access to the full NOS.

These standards are not themselves of National Vocational Qualifications (NVQs). They are however used as the structure and content of NVQs. Most of the examination boards produce the instructions and syllabuses for candidates and centres to follow in order to obtain an NVQ Level 2 or 3, and some are also producing their own awards based on these standards, which are not NVQs. NVQs are a way of achieving qualifications without taking formal examinations, where your competence is assessed by your workplace performance as well as your answers to questions about knowledge underpinning that

Table 1.1 Level 2 units and standards with chapter references

Unit no.	Unit title	Standard no.	Standard title	Main chapter sources
2-1	Help with classroom resources and records	2-1.1	Help with the organisation of the learning environment	4 with a little in 6, 7 & 10
		2-1.2	Help with classroom records	4 with a little in 2, 3 & 7
2-2	Help with the care and support of pupils	2-2.1	Help with the care and support of individual pupils	6 with some in 3, 4, 5 & 7
		2-2.2	Help with the care and support of groups of people	6 with some in 3 & 7
2-3	Provide support for learning activities	2-3.1	Support the teacher in the planning and evaluation of learning activities	7 with a little in 3, 5, 6 & 10
		2-3.2	Support the delivery of learning activities	7 with some in 2, 5, 6 & 10
2-4	Provide effective support for your colleagues	2-4.1	Maintain working relationships with colleagues	3 with a little in 2 & 4
		2-4.2	Develop your effectiveness in a support role	2
2-5	Support literacy and numeracy activities in the classroom	2-5.1	Help pupils with activities that develop literacy skills	8 with a little in 6 & 7
		2-5.2	Help pupils with activities that develop numeracy skills	8 with a little in 7
3-1	Contribute to the management of pupil behaviour	3-1.1	Promote school policies with regard to pupil behaviour	6
		3-1.2	Support the implementation of strategies to manage pupil behaviour	6
3-10	Support the maintenance of pupil safety and security	3-10.1	Contribute to the maintenance of a safe and secure learning environment	4 with some in 2, 5 & 10
		3-10.2	Minimise the risks from health emergencies	4 and 5 with a little in 2
3-11	Contribute to the health and well-being of pupils	3-11.1	Support pupils in a new setting	5
		3-11.2	Support pupils in maintaining standards of health	5 with some in 2 & 4
		3-11.3	Respond to signs of health problems	5 with a little in 2 & 4
3-17	Support the use of information and communication technology in the classroom	3-17.1	Prepare ICT equipment for use in the classroom	10 with some in 4
		3-17.2	Support the use of ICT equipment	10 with a little in 7

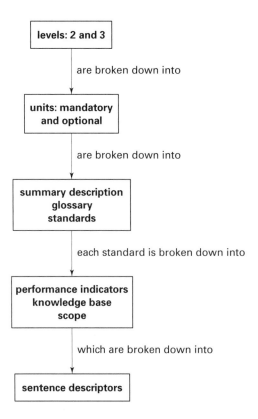

Figure 1.1 The structure of the National Occupational Standards for teaching/classroom assistants

performance. Different centres have different ways of questioning candidates, some do it verbally, others do it by assignment. You should be able to opt for the most appropriate method for your way of working. Search around your area for the further education (FE) or adult education (AE) college that is offering a course using your preferred mode of learning. Video or audio tape recording of your understanding should be acceptable if writing is difficult, although in the case of TA NVQs it is difficult to see how a candidate with writing difficulties can help pupils in literacy lessons. Whatever award you undertake, the Qualifications and Curriculum Authority (QCA) will have matched its content to these NOS.

Underpinning the NOS are a set of values and principles which have been agreed. As these are so important and fundamental to the work of TAs, they are reproduced in full at the end of this book in the Appendix. They include the expectations of TAs in their ways of working with people, pupils and the legal and local frameworks. They refer to the kind of professionalism expected of a person working in schools in a multicultural society in the twenty-first century.

2 Starting with yourself – building on induction

Study skills

Whether you want to be a really good TA or even use your experience to go on to train to be a qualified teacher, you will need to develop study skills if you do not have them already. These skills include those of personal organisation, recording, thinking about what you are doing and sharing professional ideas. You can practise observing, note-taking, reading, writing essays or accounts, finding reference books and organising your time. Try to have somewhere in your home to keep your school things – books, artefacts, your files and folders. If you do start any course of any depth you will probably need a whole shelf for the books and materials you collect, and find somewhere to study – to read or write undisturbed. TAs sometimes find themselves studying after everyone else has gone to bed, particularly if they have videos to watch as part of a course. Get some nice pens and pencils, Post-its of various sizes and a high-lighter. You will probably need ring binders, the plastic document pockets that go in them and file paper, lined in the size you are comfortable with, and a memo pad. Some TAs find themselves investing in a computer for word processing when undertaking courses if the family does not have one, but this is not essential unless you are undertaking a higher level course where typed manuscripts are mandatory. This is extremely unlikely to be the case at this level. In fact, for NVQs, tape or video recording your assessment material should be acceptable if writing is a real problem. It is really worthwhile putting in some time and thought to these practical issues and discussing them with your family; it could save some arguments or heartache later.

If organising is a problem, try indexing any collections of things that you have at home: a collection of articles, information, handouts, pamphlets on any range of topics, especially those that might be useful for school use, e.g. recipes, instructions, games with their rules or places to visit. Personal organisers can be really helpful to start with. Include a timetable of your whole day, not just your school day. When do you eat, talk with your friends or family, relax and sleep. You need to do all of these sometime, even if you do some of them at once – like talk and eat, or relax and sleep. Try to build in some time just for you, even if it is only an hour a week. Most of the other skills improve as you practise them. You might find the books on study skills by Northledge (1990) and

Freeman and Meed (1993) useful. Begin small, setting yourself realistic targets like reading a certain number of pages by the end of the week.

Local libraries can be a mine of information on what is available in your area, and may also have useful books or booklets on self-study skills. Ask for help in using the library if you are unsure where to start. The classification system they use sometimes seems designed to confuse. If you are unused to reading, try getting your speed up by reading fiction; something that grabs you will get you into a habit. Then try skimming, a most useful tool for quickly trying to find what you want – it is how most of us read the newspaper.

If writing is more of a problem, try keeping a simple diary, not just of events, but also ideas and personal comments. Try writing letters – we have all got out of this habit with the widespread use of telephones. Essay writing takes a bit more practice, and if you are feeling rusty and essay assignments are part of the course you are taking, ask for guidance. Make notes first, and then a draft. Think of whether to use sections or chapters, even put headings like this chapter, try to ensure a beginning, middle and end, and some sort of flow or continuity. Get somebody to read your draft who is prepared to offer constructive criticism before you submit a finished essay to the assessors. Note-taking is another skill, this time not using proper sentences, just clues to what you want to remember. Try making a note after a television programme of the main characters or plot as if you were going to write that letter, or of facts from a non-fiction programme. Get a good dictionary, look in the library for one you find user-friendly, and possibly a thesaurus. This is a book that groups together words with slightly differing meanings. Using one begins to extend your vocabulary.

Beware, the Internet can be a bit of a snare and a delusion if you are not used to it, as you can spend an awful lot of time (and money) searching if you do not know what you are really looking for. Again, librarians can help here and most public libraries have free access to the Net for users.

If you have a real problem with any of the skills (be honest with yourself), you could take a look at the Basic Skills courses now on offer at most adult and further education colleges and consider them before undertaking any course related to the NOS. The important thing is to get your brain working, and do something for yourself.

Keeping materials together

If you are undertaking a course it is most likely that your tutor will give you clear instructions on how to keep notes, how to study, and how best to learn and access the knowledge required of you. In case you are reading this book alone, hopefully with the support of your school mentor or a friendly class teacher, the following are a few ideas on how to proceed.

Ring binders accompanied by card pocket files are the most useful way of collecting things together. You will need a space at home to keep your papers, and the books you will begin to accumulate, such as a shelf or plastic storage box. You may need to reorganise some of your personal life to have study time away from distractions. You will need pads to write on, both A4 and note pads or exercise books for rough jottings or observations. Your tutor may talk of portfolios.

If you have been on the DfEE and DfES induction courses, you will be familiar with the personal file/portfolio that comes with the course attendance (DfEE 2000b; DfES 2001a). A detailed description of how to start a personal portfolio for yourself is given in *Assisting learning and supporting teaching* (Watkinson 2002), some of which is revisited below. You need a section purely with your personal details, and then a section for your school's details. You then can have sections for your progress in your job and for any procedure of review within your school. You can have a section for keeping your jottings or notes about courses. However, if you are studying in any depth, for an externally accredited course, such a ring file will rapidly become filled with handouts, notes on your readings, observations and other relevant materials. Such materials really need a file to themselves, separate from your personal file. This will become your reference file, or study file. For submission in an assessment process, you will need to extract materials from it and photocopy material from your personal file to produce a qualification portfolio. You cannot be assessed on materials that you have obtained from elsewhere, handouts or photocopies of pages from books, as these are the work of other people, unless you annotate them with notes about how these points are relevant to you.

Your observations of people or pupils working, comments on the reading you have done or materials or resources you have used are materials for an assessment portfolio. They show your understanding, they are evidence. One thing you should always ensure is that if you put any notes regarding pupils in your portfolio, you should anonymise or depersonalise them; that is you should refer to the pupil by a fictitious name or just a letter. 'Depersonalised information is information presented in such a way that individuals cannot be identified' (DOH, HO and DfEE 1999: 113). This also applies to any references to pupils or people in any assignments that you undertake.

A useful tip is to keep a diary or notebook with these thoughts from the beginning. This means your jottings are dated, but it does not mean you have to write something every day. Then, when you are looking for evidence, photocopy the page, highlight the relevant passage and put a reference to the NOS unit, element and section or a qualification item reference in the margin. This book is set out in that fashion, the bracketed numbers referring to the 2001 NOS (LGNTO 2001). So if you carry out any of the suggested tasks which you think might be relevant, write down what you do, what you think about the task, what you might have learnt in doing it, date the notes and if possible put the reference number as soon as you have completed it. Some time later, you can trawl through these notes for your qualification portfolio or a set assignment, and may find you have already shown competence, knowledge and understanding for many of the areas determined.

For example, by completing the following portfolio suggestions you will show that you know and understand how to develop your own effectiveness [2-4.2]. The performance indicators require that you: maintain; seek; take account of; take an active part in; undertake; and make effective use of the support available to you. Keeping a personal portfolio with dated entries should provide all the evidence you will require, to show your competence in this area. Hence the following sections are accompanied by numbers in square brackets corresponding with the NOS references on page 18 of the Level 2 standards (LGNTO 2001). If you have been on one of the induction courses mentioned above, and kept your file, you will already have most of the evidence you will need for this unit element. All you will then need to do is to relate parts of the file to the standards or assessment criteria for your award. All the induction materials are now matched to the NOS and the resultant mapping can be found on the DfES resources web site (www.teachernet.gov.uk/teachingassistants).

Contents of a personal portfolio

Keeping a note of your personal details in one place has proved to be a very useful life skill, whatever your background or expectations. We all have a birth certificate and a National Insurance number, and some of us a marriage certificate. Most of us have at least one telephone number at home and possibly also a mobile; some of us have car details or insurance details. The beginning of a personal file is just keeping these all in one place. Use the plastic pockets designed for ring files to keep documents in. This section of the file is exactly what it says – personal to you – and does not form part of your assessment portfolio unless you choose to copy things out of it. It is a place to keep those odd certificates – first aid, swimming or being a member of the winning pub quiz team. It is a place to record things you have done or learnt that are significant. All of us have achieved something; even if we left school without pieces of paper to prove it. Running clubs or a home, bringing up children or organising a meal all take skills, understanding and knowledge. If you are reading this book, you are literate. The first section may also contain your examination successes and a record of any jobs you have done, paid or voluntary. Do make sure you put dates alongside these entries. In this way, this record can be very helpful when applying for further jobs and compiling a CV (curriculum vitae, a record of your professional career).

A professional portfolio

The above collection of personal items becomes a personal/professional portfolio when you start keeping details in it from your current job. General suggestions for sections are as follows.

Section 2
Your first entry will be your job description [2-4.2:i]. While this is not a legal requirement, good management always provides one and you should ask for one. It should state: what you are required to do to support pupils, teachers, the school and the curriculum; to whom and for what you are responsible; and what the school will do to support you.

It is important that you understand your job description as to where your responsibilities not only start but finish. Your job description can define not only your TA role but also your role and responsibilities with regard to health, safety and security and there is much more about this in later chapters [3-10.1:iii]. You should always be working under the direction of a teacher, whether or not that teacher is actually present in the room with you. The final responsibility for the learning of the pupil in the school is that of a qualified teacher, whether or not you have planned the activity, prepared the materials, carried out the task and fed back what happened, whether or not it is decided that you can liaise directly with the parent or contribute to the assessment report on the pupil. Several of the standards refer to you working within the limitations of your knowledge, understanding and skills, or within the limits of your job description. It is important that you know yourself and your capabilities and do not try to undertake more than you can do, and that you only undertake things for which you have been made responsible. Nevertheless, it is hoped that you are intelligent and can use your initiative where appropriate. If you feel you can do more than you were originally employed for, talk with your line manager. In most cases senior staff will be delighted when people offer to do more, but it could be that it is actually someone else's job already, or it is inappropriate for reasons that only they can see. Often standards or job descriptions talk of 'appropriate' support or help. You have to find out what this means for you in your situation, by asking. Too often in the past things have been left to people's intuition, but it need not be so. Explicit instructions can be given and do help iron out misunderstandings before they happen.

You will then need details of the place in which you work, the context for your job. You must recognise that going to work in a school has some big differences from being at home. You will not be working on your own, but you will be part of various teams, within the classroom, the TA team and the whole school. You will be working with other people and, what is different from most other work places, you will be working with other people's children. Your relationships with these two groups are of vital importance and Chapter 3 talks about the people you work with and will enable you to understand some of the issues. You have to work within the legal context of school and the school's own policies. The policies and procedures of your school will make a difference to the way you work, and it is here that you can collect any relevant paperwork. Chapter 4 contains a lot of information as to the relevance of various school policies and procedures to the work of TAs. There will be guidance in many of the emergency, health and safety areas for you already in writing in the school in the form of policies. You must read these and discuss anything you do not understand with your line manager or mentor. Make a note of their answers and read Chapter 4 for more details.

Section 3

As circumstances change, your job will change, and so this should be reflected in changes in your job description. In addition, you are entitled to a review of your work [2-4.2:ii]. This review is called an appraisal, and should be conducted at least annually. Often people in your position, when first taken on, are likely to be subject to a period of probation, and you should be told immediately if your work is not satisfactory and helped to put any problems right during that time. It is up to you to do what is required, but most people not only want to do the minimum but also to do their best. So any review should also be an opportunity for praise – it is a performance review. Any observations of you at work for such a review should be shared with you. A record of this process can all be kept in your file. Some ideas for self-review are:

Constituents of the self-review
(This is not something that can be completed in one go. Do not tackle this all at once – try it a bit at a time.)

List your:
- Successes and appreciation from others
- Job satisfaction and lack of it – fulfilling your existing job description
- Relationships with pupils, colleagues and others associated with the school
- Understanding of the learning process and special educational needs
- Teaching skills and contribution to the learning objectives of the teachers
- Relevant curriculum knowledge and understanding
- Contributions to pastoral and physical care and behaviour management
- Understanding of and contributions to school life
- Professional development opportunities taken: training, courses, meetings attended, personal study undertaken, in school or out of school
- Setting and achieving of any personal targets
- Areas for change, development or improvement – adjustments to job description, and career development issues or ideas

(Watkinson 2002: 85)

Immediately you add things like this, you can see that you are maintaining an up-to-date record of what you are doing [2-4.2:1]. You should keep a note of any courses you attend, or school meetings – just dates and titles and maybe a brief comment on the relevance of the activity to you and your job. Keep the course handouts and meeting notes somewhere other than in your portfolio, as they are likely to become quite bulky.

Sometimes visiting advisers or inspectors comment on your work, sometimes parents or pupils write letters to you when they leave the school. Keep these letters or a note of comments (dated) in your file; they all add to the evidence of how your job is going.

Figures 2.1, 2.2 and 2.3 are taken from Maldon Primary School development portfolio for support staff.

Section 4
While the school should provide the review system, you must take account of what is said about your performance, discuss any targets suggested for you constructively, and carry out any agreed to the best of your ability [2-4.2:2, 3 & 4]. Part of the agreed targets may be to undertake more training, or attend professional development opportunities offered within the school [2-4.2:5 & iii]. Attending staff meetings about new initiatives could be suggested, for instance,

Work-Related Observation

A development portfolio meeting will occasionally be preceded by a work-related observation by a colleague. The focus of the observation will be agreed beforehand. The following proforma should be completed by the observer after an observation.

Observation of: by:

Date:

Time:

Focus:

Brief description of session:

Issues arising from session:

(Points for action will be included on target sheet)

MALDON PRIMARY SCHOOL PERFORMANCE REVIEW STATEMENT

Name of LSA
Name of performance reviewer
Date of review meeting:
Progress against previously agreed objectives
New objectives
Monitoring A short meeting to discuss progress against these objectives will be held on:
Lesson Observation
Training and Development (This section can be copied to the Staff Development Manager)

Statement agreed by...............................Date...........

MALDON PRIMARY SCHOOL

PERFORMANCE MANAGEMENT

MID-CYCLE MEETING TO DISCUSS PROGRESS AGAINST PREVIOUSLY AGREED OBJECTIVES

Name of LSA . . . .

Namer of performance reviewer . . . .

Date of meeting . . . .

Please refer to each objective in turn and outline progress made. Use an additional sheet if necessary.

Further training needs

Signed...(LSA)

Figure 2.1 (above left)   Observation page from development portfolio for support staff
© Source: Maldon Primary School, Essex

Figure 2.2 (above right)   Performance review page from development portfolio for support staff
© Source: Maldon Primary School, Essex

Figure 2.3 (below left)   Meeting page from development portfolio for support staff
© Source: Maldon Primary School, Essex

or participating in the school in-service for teachers (INSET) days. You should keep a record of ideas and opportunities offered and those that you might have come across. It is reasonable for the school to pay you for attending meetings in what otherwise would be your own time, and most schools pay for TAs to attend courses, and even finance the course fees. They see it as being in their own best interest to have highly competent and trained staff, and recognise the low pay scales on which many of you operate. However, even teachers and heads do undertake self-financed further study sometimes in their own time and for their own career enhancement, like taking Open University modules to gain a higher degree. It is always worth trying to negotiate something.

You should try and take any opportunity to develop yourself. Adults remain learners all their lives, and a school functions well when all the staff form part of a learning community. Ask questions, read relevant books or bits of them, attend area TA meetings or conferences, visit other schools if you have the opportunity. You also provide a good role model for the pupils if they know you are trying to improve yourself and learn more about the job.

You

'Knowing yourself' also includes knowing 'how to maintain your own health and safety' when dealing with pupils and 'your own capabilities to deal with an emergency' [3-10.2:vi]. You could even endanger life if you overstepped your own limitation, say in the area of first aid. For instance, if you move someone who has a broken back, it can cause untold damage, or put butter on a burn (an old-fashioned remedy), or apply a tourniquet unnecessarily or for too long.

You should take care of your own health too. It is your responsibility to stay healthy and fit, to know how or when to move things safely so as not to damage yourself, not to go crazy with gardening in the spring and make yourself unfit for work. This means eating properly and getting sufficient sleep, as well as taking normal steps if you are unwell or maintaining courses of medication prescribed for you. It means being concerned about your own habits which might be life-shortening like smoking, lack of exercise or overeating. It is your responsibility to share any health problems you might have that might affect your work, with your line manager, and that includes emotional problems as well [3-10.3:vi; 3-11.2:x & 3:viii].

Ask yourself the following:

- Do you have first aid qualifications or not? Of what sort? Are they up to date?
- Do you know what to do if a pupil you have been working with has an infectious disease like German measles, or a condition like nits?
- How do you work alongside a pupil with a heavy cold?
- How do you protect yourself appropriately when dealing with pupils who have wet or soiled themselves, cut themselves a little or are bleeding a great deal?
- What do you do if a pupil is violently sick in front of you?

- Is your own personal hygiene as good as it should be?
- Do you know the correct way to lift heavy boxes in order to avoid back problems?
- Do you know where the ladders and trolleys are kept, and when and how they should be used?
- Have you had training in the use of tools, equipment, materials or chemicals that you are asked to use?
- Do you know how to operate hoists or wheelchairs properly if they are to be used with pupils with whom you work?

Your personality

What you are is going to make a difference to how you do the job of TA. Research shows that the personality of the TA is important in how effective they are. While you cannot change yourself radically, you can recognise the traits that are useful in this job.

- Sensitivity to others, their feelings, aspirations, what interests them and what makes them work better, whether it is pupils or other staff, will enable you to enhance their strengths as well as developing your own.
- An outgoing personality, without dominating, enables you to make friends, share ideas and contribute to the teams within the school.
- Being approachable or available means that people will look to you to help, which is the essence of your job [2-3.2:4].
- Being able to go one step further than that required in any job always 'oils the wheels' of the organisation.
- Having good manners, a careful and responsible attitude to the job not only sets a good example to pupils but shows that you are someone who understands the importance of education and caring for others.
- Patience will be needed when working with slower children, kindness for those who are struggling and above all an empathy for all those who are learning – staff and pupils: you are a learner yourself.

Your role and responsibilities

You have to get to grips with your legal and organisational responsibilities [2-4.1:i]. You do have rights as an employee, but rights always bring responsibilities. It is likely that the organisational ones respecting your school will be your first practical priority, but all schools have to operate within a legal framework, so that will be dealt with first.

Legal framework

Acts of Parliament define the laws of our country, and the case histories, that is what goes on in the law courts, define how those laws should be interpreted. These laws and legal precedents can affect your human rights as a person, your employee rights and restrictions, and your health and safety. The Children Act affects how you behave with the pupils in the school. Education Acts determine what is to be taught, even at times how it should be taught and, although not in this country, when it should be taught in terms of daily or weekly routines. Recommendations are made about what ages things are best taught, tests and inspections set out to ensure that this happens, but children learn at different paces and in different ways. Codes of practice and Department for Education and Skills (DfES) Circulars also give guidance, but their implementation has to be tested by the courts. Some other Acts do impinge on schools such as the Data Protection Act.

You do not need to know these legalities in detail, but you do need to recognise that sometimes what seems an unnecessary procedure in school is actually done because the law states it shall be so. You can always question (politely) if you feel something is not appropriate; there are sometimes misinterpretations of the law or misunderstandings. This can be the case in some of the safety procedures; some can be based on assumptions or hearsay, not fact. But if in doubt, do what the teacher asks.

Employment law covers areas such as the need for all employees to have a rest room, access to toilet facilities, a break in the middle of the day, trade union membership rights and similar. Your school will have grievance and discipline procedures and pay policies [2-4.1:vi]. It should offer equal opportunities to appointments and advancement, and have contracts of employment. You have the right to claim against unfair dismissal (if it is), and to the appropriate warnings if your work is not up to scratch. Along with your rights goes the responsibility of doing your job properly, to the best of your ability. You want to know your way about, but the school needs to know where you are. Keep to your timetable and inform someone, probably in the office or your class teacher, if you have to divert from this. Always let someone know if you are ill or delayed [2-4.1:3]. You need to know what to do if the weather or public transport prevent you getting to school, but you are also responsible for trying to find child care facilities that do not interrupt your working time. If you act responsibly and honestly, you will find the school management understand when there are family emergencies [3-10.1:8 & ix].

Health and safety will affect every aspect of your work. It covers things like buildings and maintenance work within the school. Say you slipped on a newly polished floor and injured yourself on a projecting door catch, both of which should have been observed by the site manager or a health and safety officer (all schools have one), the school would be liable. If you are wearing unsuitable clothes for your job – high heels in a PE lesson, or no eyeshields when requested in a science lesson – you would be liable. It is up to all employees to inform someone appropriate if they see a potential hazard such as a tile coming loose or a hinge without screws. Some schools have a system, a book into which such observations can be entered, then someone responsible can initial and date when the item has been repaired or replaced. All the accident prevention, first aid and security procedures of the school will come under this heading and some are inspected by outside agencies such as the fire service. As an employee you must familiarise yourself with these procedures early on; for details see below.

The scope of risks, action and emergencies that you are expected to know and understand as stated in the NOS is worth checking out:

Scope of risks *resulting from:*
a. the use and maintenance of equipment
b. the use of materials or substances
c. unsafe behaviour
d. accidental breakages and spillages
e. environmental factors
f. unauthorised or suspicious person/people within the learning environment

Scope of appropriate action *to which this standard applies:*
a. taking actions consistent with your role and responsibilities
b. reporting *to* the person responsible for health and safety in the setting
c. setting off an alarm

Scope of emergencies *to which this standard applies:*
a. fire
b. evacuation of buildings
c. bomb scare
d. threat of violence

(LGNTO 2001, Level 2, p. 32)

The Children Act is less obvious in its effect upon you. It covers the areas where the upbringing of a child may prejudice the welfare of the child. Schools are *in loco parentis* (acting in place of a parent) for the time the children are in school. It covers how you treat children who are not your own, and your knowledge of any problem there might be out of school. As someone working closely, and sometimes intimately, with children and young people, you may be in a situation where the pupil reveals abuse to you or you could be accused of it.

The Education Acts cover such areas in state funded schools as the implementation of the National Curriculum (NC), the Local Management of Schools (LMS), inspection by Her Majesty's Inspectorate (HMI) and the Office for Standards in Education (Ofsted), and the assessment procedures for pupils. The Literacy and Numeracy Strategies and the Strategy for Key Stage 3 are not 'statutory', that is set up by Acts of Parliament, but schools when inspected would be expected to have implemented them or show their consultation with the Local Education Authority (LEA) as to why their school has opted out. The Code of Practice for SEN (DfES 2001a) is guidance issued to enable the best practice to be followed to implement an Education Act (1996).

Organisational procedures

Many of these are set up so that the school can fulfil its legal obligations; others are just to make the school run more smoothly for all concerned. Some are just because whoever set them up felt they would give the school certain characteristics which they wished to preserve for the school.

While you have to have a contract, job descriptions are not legally required but they are essential if everyone is to be clear about what and how they are to do their job. Similarly appraisals are only legally required for teachers, but equal opportunities and good practice recommends that *all* employees have the right to at least an annual review of their job description and some kind of review of the way they are doing the job. When you are appointed, do enquire about both of these. Most TAs get concerned about their pay and conditions of work. While these have improved, particularly the latter in the last five years, there is still a way to go. These are down to your local management. Local pay scales will have been determined by your LEA, but where you are put on the scale is a decision of your school's management, preferably with some kind of reference to your job requirements, responsibilities and capability to do the job. This may or may not include qualifications that you have. Your annual review should also include an element of reviewing your needs for professional development. All employees should have access to continuous professional development (CPD) both to increase their personal effectiveness and to ensure the needs of the school are being met.

In order that you know what the various procedures are for your school, many schools produce a handbook with them all laid out. Often this is different for teachers and support staff, as support staff do not need the curriculum details required by teachers.

The school handbook

If there is not one, do check out that you have the following information. You should have details of:

- The organisational structure of the school
- The roles and responsibilities of others
- Line management and staff support systems
- The expectations that the school has regarding your behaviour and dress
- The procedures to implement the legal requirements outlined above, especially for
  - health and safety
  - fire and accident procedures
  - first aid and security
- Relevant policies
- Communication systems
- Timetables and time allocations for planning, attendance at school events etc.
- Your roles and responsibilities including the limitations of your role

---

Much of the above sounds a bit mechanistic, but life in any organisation depends much more on the people in it. That is why many schools now look at the processes involved in becoming Investors in People (IiP). The example (Figure 2.4) of a TA policy statement has the IiP logo on it. Not so many schools actually go for the formal recognition. It is worth asking whether the school in which you work has this award and what it means to them, or if they have considered it. Whichever way it is, the relationships between the people in the school and their understanding of its aims and policies will affect the way in which you work and how effective you can be in your job. Chapter 4 deals with this aspect. Figure 2.4 indicates the range of activities and documents which can be found in a school to support the TAs (called Learning Support Assistants (LSAs) in this school). Take advantage of such support, and ensure you carry out your job description with all its associated responsibilities.

LEARNING SUPPORT ASSISTANTS

school achievement award
Department for Education and Employment

INDUCTION
• Mission and aims
• Staff Handbook
• Shadowing
• Initial training
• Job description

TRAINING AND DEVELOPMENT
• Internal – resources, cascading
• External – LSA Training, TRAC (Module 1 and 2), STAC, Dyslexia Teaching Certificate, ALS, Springboard, Graduate Teaching Programme
• Personal aspirations
• Linked to staff reviews
• Portfolio – early stages

COMMUNICATION
• Mission and Aims
• School Development Plan
• Weekly Meetings – LSAs
• Pigeon Hole – Notices and Newsletters
• Base Meetings
• Planning/Timetables
• Staff Meeting/In service
• Link Books
• Termly IEP Reviews with parents
• Rep on Governing Body

STAFF REVIEWS
• Base Leaders – held twice a year
• Opportunity to reflect and look forward
• Targets agreed and resources identified

AFFIRMATION AND SUPPORT
• Interested and value work of LSA
• Approachable and open culture
• Whole school approach to support
• We hope to make LSA work focused, supported and FUN!

INVESTOR IN PEOPLE

Figure 2.4   A TA (LSA) policy statement
© Source: Our Lady of Peace Junior School, Slough

Your personal equipment

In addition to wearing the right clothes for the purpose for which you are employed, you might like to consider equipping yourself with some of the following items. A small plastic stacker box, a toolbox with a lid or one of the open ones with a handle might be useful to carry them about the school. The school may help with providing some of the items:

A TA kit could consist of:

• Several sharp pencils
• Pencil sharpener
• Soft toilet roll or box of tissues
• Sellotape
• Ruler – the clear plastic ones are very useful

- Red, black and blue biros
- Stapler
- Hole punch
- Scrap paper for pupils to try out spellings on
- Small memo pad
- Small and large pairs of scissors
- Two rubbers
- Paperclips
- Card folder to keep your papers in
- Clipboard with timetable and any planning sheets

You will soon find you are carrying children's work around, or odd books as well, so a large strong carrying bag or box will also be useful. Some general TA books may already be available in your school and are worth dipping into as well as using this one (Fox 1998; Balshaw 1999; Watkinson 2002).

3 Working in the school team

It is possible that you have come into the job of TA by answering an advertisement in a local shop or paper or even, hopefully, some of the readers are young people looking for a worthwhile career. Traditionally, people have come into the job through being known to the school, often helping in a voluntary capacity or employed as a midday assistant. In this latter case, the head or a senior manager spotted you and may have offered you a paid job in class for a few hours supporting a child with SEN. Secondary TAs may have followed pupils with SEN as they progressed into the upper phases from primary school. All of you will have been to school, and many of you are parents with children either at school or who have been through the system. It is tempting to think because of your previous experiences, you know all about how schools work. But being an employee, part of a workforce in a particular setting, does bring different perspectives, responsibilities, needs and support. All schools are different, not just because of their locations, geographical layout or phase but because of the particular gel of that group of people. Working with this group of people has similarities to working in any team or organisation, but schools also have their own legal and organisational framework, as well as developing their own ethos and culture. Relationships between all the people concerned are important, and even if you feel that you are only going to relate to a few pupils and one or two teachers, understanding the complexity of the whole-school community is essential to ensuring you achieve the best for those with whom you come into close contact. By the whole-school community, I mean the pupils and their parents, the teachers and support staff, the governors and the local community including the visiting advisers from the various authorities associated with a school.

You have a responsibility to get to know who is who, who does what and when, recognising the local and national framework within which you work, but you also need to give of yourself to the people with whom you work, to make relationships that will create working partnerships, and be part of various teams – the whole-school team as well as your own TA team or curriculum support team. You will need to recognise how the policies and practice of those around you affect you and how you will affect them and their work.

The good thing is that the school also has a responsibility to support you. Increasingly senior managers and class teachers are realising that a TA does not just happen, or appear from time to time, but given the appropriate employment support and personal and professional support can become one of the most treasured resources of the school. Being supported by the school, participating in the various activities – in-house training, meetings, reviews and social events – you will become part of the team. Schools work best where they are collegial, that is people work together for a common good, each one knowing how they fit into the whole. In this way you will receive and give friendship and increase your job satisfaction. As time goes on this will become a critical friendship. This is a term used in schools to indicate professional partnerships, which not only work but are growing through the partners being able to comment appropriately on how they are working together. It does not mean you will become critical in a denigratory way of all around you, or they of you, but that you become able to take and give constructive suggestions for improvement.

The basic principles of good relationships

There are some principles that underlie good relationships whether they are professional or social, to do with friendships or the work place, whether within lifelong partnerships like marriage or a temporary job [2-4.1:ii]. Basically it boils down to treating others as you would like to be treated, putting yourself metaphorically in the other's shoes. Having respect for the other person or people in the relationship will show itself in things like good manners, listening when others talk, reading messages and notices, being prepared to give and take [2-2.2:3]. Good manners can have a cultural side to them, for instance using 'please' in some cultures is a sign of pleading not politeness. Good relationships are built on a sensitivity to such differences. A mutual trust has to be built up. All those concerned in a relationship are interdependent in some way even if it seems like a very power-heavy relationship. Even these need the cooperation of the participants to work or there will be anarchy. You may have rights but you also have responsibilities; you have a certain commitment even if it is short-term. Where relationships are effective, there is a mutual accountability, whether doing the asking or being asked to complete a task of some kind.

Simple things like punctuality, truthfulness, honesty and reliability build up the necessary trust [2-4.1:2]. Be prepared to apologise and recognise your own mistakes, and try not to repeat them. Effective communication is essential in good relationships. This not only means listening, but also giving clear, appropriate and if possible unambiguous instructions or messages; even simple things like not mumbling when in doubt will help. Be explicit (politely) about needs and misunderstandings; implicit messages can be misunderstood, causing hurt or delay. Write things down for yourself and others where you can, being as concise as possible. Ordinary conversational rules apply such as allowing others to get a word in, yet standing firm when you are sure – assertive without being aggressive.

Maintaining positive attitudes such as trying to see the good in people or pupils, trying to understand, smiling where you can, all help relationships to work. Ask for things in a positive not a negative manner, give instructions similarly. Try to thank people for things wherever possible, without being a 'creep'. Good relationships use systems of collaboration rather then conflict, although this does not mean always agreeing with others. Your 'yes' is only as good as your 'no', that is, only agree to do what you know you can achieve, otherwise people will not trust you. Avoid damaging conflict and unnecessary confrontation. Aggression and attention-seeking do not get the same results as cooperation. If you have a problem, share it and do not let it fester. If in doubt, ask.

In organisations, there will be some kind of leadership. This may reside in one person, who then delegates down through a largely hierarchical network, or it can be a flatter organisation where more people take collaborative decisions. You will need to find out how your school operates. Historically schools have been hierarchical, with a head teacher, a deputy, a senior management team, teachers and the support staff, but many schools have tried to share leadership, giving responsibilities to others. In all relationships, there are roles and some kind of rules, whether written or not. Collaborative cultures do take more effort on the part of everyone in them, but have been found to produce more effective organisations. They prevent fragmentation of jobs and duplication, which has a beneficial effect on the pupils.

Think of a hotel or a shop that you know quite well where you feel well served.

- Do they know to whom to go if they cannot answer your query?
- Do they seem sure of their own role?
- Can they direct you to the appropriate service if they are busy?
- Do the staff know what other people on the staff do?
- Are they polite, interested in their job and you?

- Why do you go back to that establishment?

The important relationships in a school

There are various professional relationships of which you will become part once you start working in the school [2-4.1:vii]. Being a professional may be a new concept to you. It is important that you do not treat colleagues like you would a friend or member of your family, particularly at first. You may have been working in a playgroup, where the children call you by your first name and treat you like an auntie. The people you worked with may well have been your neighbours or people you met in the antenatal class. The tendency with friends is to chat while on the job, make excuses for mistakes and take things for granted because you know them well. Once working in a school certain things will be expected of you in your relationships. You should not chat on the job, you should always try to carry out tasks to your best ability, and you should be reliable and punctual. You must be very careful what you discuss about what goes on in the school outside with friends or family. Forming relationships with pupils and adults is like taking one step back from familiarity. This does not mean you are cold, withdrawn or stand-offish. Nor does it mean you do not make friendships with any school staff which continue out of school. It is about maintaining a balance, being friendly and approachable even to those people you may dislike – and there could be some.

Think of various places where you have contact with others in a professional capacity

- A supermarket
  Do you like it when: the cashier talks to her colleague and not to you?
  The shelf stackers get in the way of your trolley and think their job is more important?
  Customer services promises to ring you back about a query and never does?
- A hotel
  Do you like it when: the receptionist chats to each customer so long that you are kept waiting?
  The waiter is careless with serving?
  The bill is incorrect and the discussion with the manager about it takes place in front of everyone else?
- A hospital
  Do you like it when: the receptionist cannot find your paperwork?
  The machine operative turns up late after lunch?
  The equipment the doctor needs is not clean or readily available, and you have to wait while they sort it out?
  You feel the staff may be laughing at your condition?
- A shop
  Do you like it when: staff training about using a credit card to pay for goods takes place in front of you, on the job?
  Order promises are not kept?
  The assistant asks you irrelevant personal questions?
- Can you think of similar situations in your school, how you could and should behave in the various circumstances?

This section deals with each relationship in turn.

Working closely with individual or small groups of pupils

You will be given a few pupils or possibly even one with whom the school want you to work particularly [2-2.1:2]. The relationship with them is crucial. This is not a parent–child relationship although at times it may come to feel like it, especially where the pupil is physically impaired to the extent that you have to perform some intimate tasks for them. It must remain professional without becoming distant. One TA described their aim as 'to do myself out of a job'. Hopefully as the pupils get older and mature, they will be able to do more and more for themselves. This immediately means that you will need advice about how far you go in supporting that pupil, how it is best for you to intervene and when to stand back, what to do with your time if you are standing back, who you tell if things change, what your relationships to the pupils' parents are and so on. It means you need to know what the teacher's intentions are for that pupil; what you should do if things get out of hand – what the policy is for managing difficult behaviour; what you do if the pupil tells you things that worry you – what is the child protection policy; what to do if the pupil cannot do the task to which you have been allotted – what is the SEN policy; and who you can talk to about the whole situation – the confidentiality policy. You can see, there is a lot to learn.

Case study: A good working relationship with a pupil

Sandra, a TA in a primary school, had been appointed to look after Jo, a child starting school, who was still not fully toilet-trained. Jo also had some learning problems and had been slow in reaching most of his physical development milestones. Both his parents were agreed they wanted him to go to the local mainstream school, and had sought help early from the local authority. Sandra talked with Jo when he first came into school and met his mother to find out about how she dealt with the toilet-training. She made sure that Jo knew how he could attract her attention if she was not working alongside him, should he feel the need of her help. She agreed these signals with his class teacher. When in class with Jo, Sandra did many other tasks for the teacher with other children, but kept to a regular timetable with Jo, again agreed with his teacher. At these times, she and Jo departed quietly for the toilet area. During this time, whatever Jo's physical needs, she talked with him about his interests both in and out of school and listened to him. She let him return to class on his own, to help him keep his sense of self-esteem. She used the same language as his mother for bodily parts and functions and she kept a 'weather ear' open in class and the playground to see if the other children were ever 'taking the Mickey' out of him or surreptitiously bullying him. She praised his successes in the training routines and ignored the failures, but dealt with them quietly and appropriately. Her aim was to gain Jo's confidence, yet create as much independence for him as possible. She needed to balance his need for adult help with his need to retain self-respect, especially in front of his friends and peers.

When you have a new pupil to work with of whatever age:

- Use the first name by which he or she wishes to be known.
- Make sure they know your name in school. This should be your title (Mr, Mrs or Miss) and your family name.
- It is preferable to have pupils use this name, not your first name or 'Miss'/'Sir'. If the norm is for the teachers to be addressed in this way, discuss the issue politely with your line manager or a senior manager. Mutual self-respect in using names like this helps keep the relationship on a professional yet familiar footing.
- Find out from the teachers why you have been assigned to the pupil.
- Talk with the pupil away from the classroom about your role, be open about what you aim to do, and help them be open with you about their likes and dislikes.

- Always try to let them do something for themselves.
- Praise where praise is due; do not give empty praise, they always know.
- Always treat them with respect, yet ensure you follow the school guide-lines for behaviour management and other relevant policies. Just because you may be working with them on a one-to-one basis is no excuse for different rules.
- Keep in close communication with the class teachers and specialist teachers who introduced the pupil to you in the first place so that you know what you are supposed to be doing, why and whom to tell if circumstances change.

One of the problems – or it can be a joy – of working at a school near where you live is that you will meet pupils out of school hours. Younger pupils, usually accompanied by a familiar adult, will greet you like a long lost friend, introduce you to whoever they are with and want to chat. While this can be endearing, it can be a trial, if the child becomes too familiar with you or cling-ing or creates a jealousy within a carer, particularly if it is the mother who has found the child difficult to handle. Older pupils may do the opposite and pretend, particularly if they are with their peers, that they do not know you. If there is a problem, share it with the pupil when you are next in a quiet place together in school and ask how you can best resolve it together.

Another thing to watch out for is becoming too fond of your charge. This may not be a problem, but it could prevent you wanting to hand over responsibility for them to another TA or seeing them move from your care in a primary school to a secondary school. This is where there is a clear difference between the kind of care you can give and that of a parent. You need to be able to let go if appro-priate, and move on. Sometimes this bond can be long lasting as well as quite professional, and blossom into genuine friendship in later life outside school, with you becoming a surrogate aunt or uncle, but this is infrequent. One of the scenarios I have often come across is where the TA has moved from working in the local playgroup to working in school as their own children get older. Many of the children know the TA therefore, but are used to treating them as 'mum's friend' or always using first names and showing considerable familiarity. While this may seem like forging good relationships, it is really too cosy for school, and you need to create just a little more distance and professionalism.

Partnership with teachers

Whatever you do in school should be under the direction of a qualified teacher. The status conferred on them by their qualifications does mean taking respon-sibility for the learning of pupils whether in a class or a subject. This respon-sibility includes managing other adults in the classroom to support that learning. However, you will often find yourself doing tasks that include teach-ing or working with a small group out of the sight of the class teacher. Whatever the situation, that teacher still takes responsibility for the progress of the pupils and for ensuring that your role with them is as effective as possible. This can create tensions with the teacher; either you feel underused or you are given more responsibility than you feel comfortable with.

The secret lies in the relationship with the teacher [2-3.1:i]. It has to be a professional partnership, with good communication and a clear understanding of the boundaries within which you operate. This means being explicit about how things are working, not accepting the implicit. You or the teacher may be wrong in making assumptions about situations. Once a good working relationship is established with lines of communication, you may not need to meet daily or plan specific tasks.

You will find, even in the same school, that each teacher has their own foibles, and you as a TA are likely to work with several in a week or possibly even in a day. Many schools have realised that allowing the teacher and TA continuous time together, even in some cases allocating one TA per class in a primary school, has a beneficial effect on working relationships. On the other hand, varied experiences and working with different adults can increase your understanding of the different ways of tackling similar problems, giving you a range of ideas of how to operate.

Relationships take time and thought, they do not just happen, particularly if two people are put together to work who have little else in common. It is important that you take time to talk with and listen to the teachers you work with, spend out-of-class contact time with them, if only in the corridor on the way to or leaving a lesson. Normal chat about the weather, families, homes or hobbies can cement relationships and prove to each partner that the other is human. The school should allow you to use the same staffroom as the teachers, although this is occasionally a problem where space is at a premium. Similarly, cloakrooms, toilet areas, car parks, all provide common ground for beginning conversations. On top of this, the school should also ensure that you both have non-class contact time to discuss curriculum matters and pupils' needs properly, to plan together what needs to be done. There is much more about this professional side of the relationship in the chapter on supporting the teacher.

Case study: A good relationship with a teacher

TA Kati is working in a secondary school, particularly employed to support Hassan who has learning needs. Kati is line managed by the teacher coordinating SEN (the SENCO), and has met regularly with her and the team. She is clear about her tasks with Hassan, and attends most lessons with him. She is particularly interested in English, partly through her own interest in the subject, but also because of Hassan's learning problems. His reading and writing is behind what it should be, although his spoken English is fluent and extensive. After English lessons she had walked with John, the teacher, to the staffroom and got into conversation with him about how best to help Hassan. Her own love of language has come out in the conversations, and John has lent her books – both fiction which extends her own reading range, and non-fiction about the teaching of reading and writing to those with Hassan's needs. John encouraged Kati to go to the local FE college to take her A level English, something she had not contemplated previously, leaving school at 16. Kati was able to recommend a local playgroup for John's growing family. When they both attended a course on partnership, they talked of Kati's support during a stressful Ofsted inspection and John's career advice. Kati was beginning to consider that she may go on to train as a teacher.

When starting with a new teacher, a simple checklist may be useful.

Some questions you could ask before going into a different teacher's classroom

- What do you particularly want me to do?
- What do I do if a pupil in your room asks to go to the toilet?
- Can I write in any pupils' books?
- What contact with parents or carers do you expect of the TA?
- Do you want me to attend consultation evenings?
- Do I take part in SEN reviews?
- Can I do anything at the request of a parent, such as change a child's reading book or search for lost equipment?
- Can I tidy the rooms? Your desks? The resources area?
- Is there anything you do *not* want me to do?   (Watkinson 2002: 63)

Working as a support staff member, part of a whole-school team

You will be part of a team of adults who have all sorts of roles and responsibilities. This is quite different from being a member of a class at school, where you all seemed to be part of a group with the teacher on the opposite side. Nor do schools work like offices or factories, where each has a role, and often what people do in one part of the organisation has little apparent meaning or effect on others. Even in a large secondary school, where the teaching staff alone can number 100 people, and support staff at least that again, the efficiency and effectiveness for the pupils is better where these people work as a team. Sometimes people have drawn images of schools as a ship, with a captain, crew, passengers and so on, sometimes as a garden centre where different plants can grow, needing different cultivation conditions and methods, or as a stage with actors out front and backstage hands supporting their work. In the past schools were often staffed according to a strict pupil–teacher formula and the teaching staff were all that apparently counted when head teachers referred to 'their staff'. This culture is passing and there is much greater recognition that all staff have a role to play and their effectiveness affects the effectiveness of other members of staff. As a member of the support staff, you provide the foundation on which the teachers can lean.

In order to make the whole staff operate as a team, some schools even go to the length of making everyone go on a 'team building exercise' such as one sometimes sees in advertisements or films. More make it explicit that operating as a team is important, and a few just ignore it. Teams need every member to play a part, to know when to put themselves forward for tasks and when to take instructions from others. This takes thought and sometimes patience or initiative. It will be for you to be sensitive and judge how best you can be a team member in your school. This means you need to know where you fit in in any hierarchy, who does what and when, how the systems and structures of your school work for communication and consultation [2-4.1:iv]. These are dealt with in greater detail below. You need to try to put as many faces to names as possible, and get to know them when you can. Do join in events and social occasions when you can, which will be in your own unpaid time. Even going to school fêtes or bazaars can help you find a place, showing you want to cooperate, to belong to the school.

Watching a team working in sport or planning an event, you can see how roles develop. Somebody will probably be a leader, some seem just followers, even sleeping partners. Some apparently quiet people turn out to be the reliable ones who do the tasks others have set conscientiously and without complaining; others make a lot of fuss, yet rarely achieve the aims of the group; some are good at ideas but awful at carrying them out; some can be bossy; and some quite content to 'go with the flow'. An ideal team person can listen, yet contribute when they have something to say or do, and help others achieve their tasks. What are you?

Being part of a TA team

Secondary schools have developed the idea of TA teams more fully, understanding that TAs are very unlikely to stay with one teacher for the whole time, unless they are operating in a small department as a technician, such as in science, design and technology (DT) or information and communications technology (ICT). Most primary schools do have more than one TA, even in the smallest schools, so you are likely to be part of such a group. This itself is a team. You will be doing similar types of jobs although likely to be with different pupils or age groups or in secondary possibly supporting different curriculum areas. This means you can form relationships with people who may have similar problems and joys to yourself and probably similar training needs, at least where supporting your particular school is concerned.

You may have totally different backgrounds or qualifications but you will all be part of your school team [2-4.1:1]. Thus training together for new initiatives within the school makes sense, sharing resources and ideas, or even just being there for each other if personal things get a bit tough. You can support your colleagues and be supported by them. By training and meeting together as a team you are part of the learning community which is a school.

Roles and responsibilities

Ethical expectations

It is expected that you as an employee will abide by the expectations outlined in the handbook list given in Chapter 2. If there is a dress code, there will be a reason for it. Sometimes it will be for your safety, sometimes it is to reinforce the ethos of the school. It may be for instance that the school considers that respect and tidiness in staff set standards and provide a role model for pupils. All adults in a school offer a role model in their dress and behaviour as to how pupils can and should behave, and what being an adult is like [2-2.2:iv].

The whole question of ethos is a difficult one to grasp; it is not often explicit, except in some religious schools, but it is about the climate and tone the school is trying to promote [2-4.1:v]. It will include things like respect for individuals, expectations of behaviour, positive attitudes towards each other and the appropriate use of praise, a sense of identity and pride in the school, a recognition of the importance of the environment, effective communications and relationships, and a willingness of people to be involved in voluntary things on behalf of the school. None of these are legal or organisational requirements, but they go to making the school a better place to be, and in which to learn.

Along with ethos goes the principle of quality. You should give of your best to provide the best kind of environment for learning to enable both pupils and other adults to give of their best. Personal qualities such as honesty and trust are required. For instance, if you are asked to pass on a message from a teacher to the office staff, this should be done promptly and accurately, yet recognising when is an appropriate moment to do it. An office with a visiting parent in is not the time to announce the particular need for support to another pupil. Written notes should be treated as written records, and should be accurate, concise, dated and legible, and treated as a confidential document unless you know otherwise [2-1.2:4]. If you want to be treated as an equal you must ensure that you give the pupils you work with equal opportunities to succeed, not favouring one over another. This does not mean you give them all equal time or the same task or the same resources – the crucial word is 'opportunity'.

This principle leads to that of inclusion. It has been found that most pupils with SEN succeed better when they are included in the curriculum provided for pupils with fewer needs, so long as specialist provision is made for special needs where this takes place. How those needs are met does not necessarily mean withdrawal from mainstream classrooms or mainstream schools. Nor do statements like the above mean that there should be no withdrawal from classes and no special schools. It means that segregation socially or educationally needs to be considered seriously as to whether it is providing the best for the pupil *and* giving them an equal opportunity to succeed in a variety of contexts.

Another principle that underpins practice in schools is that of celebrating diversity [2-3.1:ii]. We are lucky in many of our schools to have pupils from many backgrounds and many cultures, thus opening up the opportunity for sharing and richness that is not otherwise easily available. Pupils in a predominantly white area may have seen establishments such as 'take-aways' in the shopping precinct as the only differences around. They will not have the opportunity to see the richly patterned fabrics of saris or hear music on African instruments, to see the interesting formations of Chinese or Arabic scripts on books or buildings unless staff make arrangements for them to do so. Pupils in wheelchairs could be the best artists in the class, and one having difficulty in reading could be the best footballer. Working in a school means being on a lookout to see opportunities for enjoyment in everything around you, and sharing them with others.

Enquire what ethnic mix comes to your school.

- Are different languages spoken at home or in the school?
- What books are available in the school to show different cultures and ways of life?
- Are there books that show people with disabilities as heroes?
- What resources in terms of musical instruments, fabrics, pictures or artefacts does the school have?
- What recorded music is played in the school and is only Western art displayed on the walls?
- What facilities are there to accommodate differences in dress worn for cultural reasons – head covering for girls or turbans for boys?
- What is the ethnic or linguistic mix of staff?
- What relationships does the school have with the local community organisations, churches or other places of worship?
- What advisers or resources outside the school are available to the school to support understanding of multicultural diversity?

Some schools have what is called a 'vision statement', which is a way of explicitly recognising what the school stands for in as succinct a way as possible. This will appear in the school's prospectus and other significant documentation. Some schools even set out the vision on the wall near the entrance to the school. Whether the vision is set out in this explicit way or not, all schools have aims about their purpose. These will usually include statements about high expectations in academic terms, about pupils' achievements, sometimes standards of behaviour or other aspects of the ethos mentioned above. When you join a school staff, you are, in a manner of speaking, 'signing up' to these expectations. Sometimes there are opportunities to discuss the statements or even revise them and as a member of staff you would be expected to contribute to such discussion.

Following these written or unwritten principles shows that you are, as an employee of the school, a professional. This means that you will do what is required to the best of your ability, developing your skills, knowledge and understanding to improve where you can. It may mean while you are at work, putting personal problems to one side, even acting a part to cover up your feelings. If there is a problem that you cannot cope with, then you must tell someone about it, so early on you need to know who your line manager is. It shows that you are committed to your job.

It can happen that with all the policies and goodwill in the world, things can go wrong for you in your working relationships in school [2-4.1:vi]. You need to be able to handle this appropriately. One of the school's policies, the *Discipline and grievance policy*, will deal with the formal way of dealing with such a problem but hopefully you never have to use this or have it used against you. There may be people you do not like, but you can do little about this in a work situation. If such a personal feeling does interfere with your work, say something has happened outside school with one of your children or a spouse or partner, which make working relationships impossible, tell your line manager in confidence. It should be possible for timetables to be adjusted.

Difficult situations

The same would apply to your finding out about dishonesty, or even malpractice of any kind – tell your line manager and let a senior colleague deal with it [2-4.1:4,5]. If you feel you are a victim of unfairness, always try the line manager route first, failing that a deputy head or even the head verbally. Formal written complaints should not be necessary. If it does come to formalities, you would be very wise to join a union and consult their people before embarking on such a procedure, and making sure you have their representative, or another colleague whom you can trust, present with you at any meetings. Keep copies of any written communication.

Such occurrences are so rare and inevitably sensitive that simulation of such situations is accepted as evidence of experience in building an award portfolio for this kind of item. The standards also refer to support networks, resources and people who can help you to deal with improving work relationships. If this area worries you at all, make sure you mention it at an early opportunity with a mentor, someone with whom you can share your fears, but who is more experienced in the ways of the school. Most of the difficult situations which you will encounter in school will be due to problems with relationships. Pupils' problems usually can be traced to their problems with each other or their families, making life hard to cope with. Managing challenging behaviour by adults is much easier where normal relationships between adults and pupils in the school are good.

Remember that by the time you have completed an induction year, you will be much more knowledgeable and experienced, and could offer support to others coming to the job after you. Make the opportunity in any job review to discuss the other person's perception of how you are fitting into the school, and add a few notes of their comments to your evidence file.

4 The school structures, systems and procedures that you need to know and understand

Policies

In order to maintain consistency across the school, the school staff develop policies. Most of the elements of the NOS refer to knowing the school policy in the area being described. Some of these are legal requirements, like having a policy on sex education, others are guidance on procedures like behaviour management and others are there to safeguard the school against unfair allegations. If parents send their children to a school where a certain policy is in place, say for dealing with bullying, and then complain about what happens, if that incident was dealt with according to the laid down policy, the parents have no grounds for complaint. They can still lobby for change, but not blame the school for dealing with the incident in the way laid down by the policy. Policies are to ensure that pupils and staff are treated the same. No member of staff can complain, 'It is no good me telling them not to slide down the banisters if the deputy head does not check them!'

You must ensure that you are given copies of the most important policies which will cover areas of your work, and that you know where you can see copies of all the others. The whole collection will be considerable and you will not need many of these. The possible content and implications for some general ones are discussed below and others concerning pupils, teaching or the curriculum are discussed in the later chapters. You will need to discuss these with your mentor or line manager, particularly where they refer to the methods to be used. Annotate your copies with a highlighter and notes as to where items especially apply to you.

The essential policies for TAs

- Any vision statement for the school or statement of faith or principles set out by the school
- Health and safety which covers:
  - General and school
  - Health and hygiene
  - Safety and security
  - Child protection

- Behaviour management which covers:
  - What constitutes 'bad' behaviour
  - Rewards and sanctions
  - Supervision
  - Restraint procedures
- SEN which covers:
  - Individual Education Plans
  - Inclusion and access
  - Independent learning
- Any TA policy or support staff policy
- Any employee policy covering items such as:
  - Pay, appraisal, consultation
  - Discipline and grievance
- Teaching and learning – general principles
- Equal opportunities, dealing with discrimination and celebrating diversity which includes:
  - Dealing with racism
  - Multiculturalism
- Curriculum areas that you support in depth, e.g. English or mathematics

Systems and procedures

Most of these will be covered by the policies mentioned above, but schools like many organisations have their customs which are not explicit, or laid down on paper and often you have to pick these up as you go along. Be observant and sensitive.

Case study: Good practice in two schools

Fairfax Primary School is in a town having 20 or so primary schools and two secondary schools. It is a town with high unemployment and considerable social problems. Fairfax serves one of the more run-down areas. Arriving at the school by car, it is clear where to park and where the pedestrian entrance is. At this entrance, there is a polite notice about directing all visitors and parents to the reception office and keeping the gate closed for small children's safety. At the office the receptionist is on the telephone but catches the visitor's eye and signals 'be with you in a minute' with a smile and a lift of the finger. The visitor is then treated courteously, offered a cup of tea as the head is busy. The seats to which one is shown are surrounded by children's work, books and magazines, a copy of the school prospectus, all tidy and clean. In the same area are photographs of all the staff and governors who are named, and given a job title. Contact telephone numbers are given for the governors. A noticeboard for parents giving forthcoming events and a recent newsletter is also in this reception area. Children walking past individually are purposeful and generally well behaved and polite. A child in the class walking past starts to push. They are changed for PE, the teacher is wearing plimsolls. He quietly asks the child to stop, explaining that that is how accidents happen. When the class reaches the destination hall, the same member of staff thanks the class for walking sensibly. Discussion with the head teacher, teachers and TAs gives consistent messages: the children attending the school come to them undisciplined, scoring poorly on entry tests; all staff are clear about their aims, what they do about problems with children or the building, resources or any other matter – they ask someone and can name to whom they go; they talk of the 'Fairfax way'. The head speaks of the years over which she has built up the team, how she selects staff and how she encourages them, allows them their say, but how she is clear what she is aiming for. The inspection report indicates considerable improvement in attainment for the pupils while they are at the school. The school is oversubscribed.

Strand Secondary School is the only secondary school in a small, fairly prosperous town. It too is oversubscribed, parents driving their children for up to eight miles to get them into the school. It is large, consistently ten form entry, that is up to 300 children start each year. This could be a logistical and communication nightmare, particularly as the school also houses local community facilities for adult education. However, many of the characteristics of the previous primary school are present: the clear signs, the welcoming staff, the notices and seating, the cleanliness and order. When directions are needed to visit the particular member of staff to be interviewed, a passing student is asked to guide the visitor to their destination. All the students are in uniform. The corridors are full of students' work and the guide points out the achievement photographs as one passes. The receiving teacher, after the guide has departed, tells the visitor of his many problems, which had not been apparent during the walk through the school. This teacher is surrounded by books, files, paper and notes of various kinds and is often interrupted during the visit. She remains calm, diverts enquiries where necessary and gives information where she has it. Data is readily available where needed, and staff including TAs brought into the conversation where appropriate. Again talking to staff individually about what they do and why provides a consistent picture of people who know where they are going together.

Both schools have a pattern of meetings and consultation, with a considerable number of regularly reviewed policies, and consistent staff behaviour towards each other and the pupils. The documentation when examined reveals written guidance for many aspects of school life, which has been put together jointly, widely circulated and there is an expectation that it will be adhered to. The result for the pupils in both schools is that they know what is expected of them and what will happen if they do not conform. They also know that well-produced work and polite behaviour is appreciated.

It is up to you to familiarise yourself with the relevant documents, ask for them if you do not have them and abide by their contents. If you do not like what you read, then participate in the meetings and consultation procedures and change things gradually and democratically. Remember there is usually a reason why the policies and procedures are as they are and you are possibly the newest member of staff. Good schools welcome new ideas and open debate but aggressive criticism does not 'win friends and influence people'.

Areas you must find out about

If there is not written guidance about any of the following in the checklist, then make sure you ask about them. This area will include the use of spaces, materials or equipment and how you should behave in different circumstances. Make a note of any items that are not already in writing and keep for reference. Highlight or mark items on the written guidance that you feel are important or wish to query. Some of them are explained in principle in the paragraphs following the list; many of them will have details that refer to your school only. If you move from one school to another, you will find there are differences in procedures of which you need to take note.

A checklist

Do you know about the following?

- Health and safety
  - Emergency and accident procedures
  - General health and hygiene matters
  - Health education policy
  - Child protection
  - Dealing with harassment and racist incidents
- Using the office
  - Other staff and equipment
  - Personal equipment and insurance
- Communication
  - Verbal and paper
  - Meetings, newsletters, staffroom, noticeboards
  - Non-verbal
  - Confidentiality
- The learning environment
  - Resources, equipment and materials,
    (general, curriculum-specific, written)
    - Preparation requirements of teacher
    - Returning correctly – storage, location
    - Monitoring
    - Checking and care
    - Making
    - Involving pupils
    - Safety equipment
    - Specific: ICT, AVA support and science, DT and art
    - School buildings and grounds
- Records
  - Storage
  - Security
  - Data protection
- School Development Plan (SDP)
  - Objectives and priorities
  - Consultation

Health and safety

All employees have a duty to observe the in-house organisational requirements in this area [3-10.1-i, 3-10.2-6]. There is considerable legislation governing health and safety at work, based on the 1974 Act and subsequent legislation such as the Management of Health and Safety at Work Regulations, 1992. These indicate that establishments must have health and safety policies and carry out risk assessments for people, equipment and off-site activities. It puts the responsibility for health and safety on employers which in the case of schools may be the LEA, the governing body, trustees or owners depending on what type of school it is. The Health and Safety Executive produce some useful information leaflets and have local offices. However, all employees have a responsibility to observe local policies and take all reasonable precautions to keep themselves and others using the premises safe. This includes being personally vigilant for potential risks to adults or pupils. It does not mean you necessarily have to mend things, or make things safe on your own, but you need to ensure that pupils in your care observe proper procedures. Your responsibilities regarding health and safety may be spelt out in your job description [2-2.1:vii]. The requirements for all staff in the areas of health, safety, security and supervision will be spelt out in writing somewhere [2-1.1:vii].

All schools will have an appointed Health and Safety Officer among the staff, usually a teacher, often linked with union affiliation. They will advise you if you have queries, or take concerns to the appropriate quarter, if you have any. The standards provide useful checklists of areas that you must attend to and find out about in your particular school. For instance, the scope of safety equipment indicates that you should know about the location of first aid boxes, how to protect children and adults against accidents and how to use different equipment in emergencies (LGNTO 2001: 5). The standards apply to all pupils whatever their special needs, all colleagues and other adults or children who may be in the building, and to all areas of the school: in and out of the classroom, outside the school buildings and in places you might visit with pupils on an educational trip (LGNTO 2001, Level 2, p. 31).

Even if you are not undertaking these units for accreditation purposes you should read the following and undertake some of the tasks [3-10.1:1]. These items are required of all employees either by law [3-10.1:ii] or for the protection of all the people within the organisation. Matters of health education, caring for individual pupils and child protection issues are dealt with in the next chapter.

Emergency and accident procedures

Before you even go to a classroom, you should know about fire alarms and procedures [2-1.1:iv; 3-10.1:x]. This includes how to evacuate the building, what to do if there is a bomb scare or an intruder. As a visitor to the school, you are usually asked to sign in so that the responsible people know who is in the building if there is an emergency. As a member of staff, it is assumed that you are on the premises if the timetable indicates such. You need to familiarise yourself with the fire alarm points, the whereabouts of extinguishers and fire blankets and their use. Remember if you are in laboratories or where different hazardous liquids are about, there may be different kinds of extinguisher in use [3-10.1:xi]. Water should not be put on oil or electrical fires as it can make matters far worse. Carbon dioxide extinguishers or fire blankets will be available in vulnerable situations; check out how and when they should be used.

Usually the fire alarm is the signal for any evacuation of the building, whatever the cause. You need to ensure any pupils in your charge behave appropriately at such times, 'silence' and 'walking only' usually being paramount. Both of these reduce panic as well as being something positive to maintain. All rooms should have evacuation instructions. If they do not, tell someone in the office – possibly pranksters have been at work.

If you are appointed to support a pupil with special physical needs, do ensure you know where all their equipment is, and what you do with them in emergencies. These could be personal to them or arise in an evacuation procedure. A wheelchair may need a special route out of some areas, like access to a lift. Alert the SENCO if you have any worries.

First aid

All schools will have at least one appointed person responsible for ensuring correct procedures are followed and probably a trained first-aider. You need to find out who these people are and where they may be found at different times of the day. Cover of some kind should be available at all times when people are on the school premises. You do not need to have first aid training but it helps, and schools usually have simple sessions every so often which deal with resuscitation, choking, bleeding and other simple procedures which anyone can use. Be wary of getting information from the Internet or books on home medicine unless you are sure of their validity, since some methods are not helpful. The Red Cross and St John's Ambulance associations run lots of courses in any community and usually will come to a specific venue to run a course if sufficient people are interested. Of course, they have a small cost. The school will have a designated first-aider who will at least have some of this training, and you will be told when and how you should use them [2-2.1:viii; 3-10.2:iii]. Common sense and experience, particularly of bringing up a family, can help you, but you must know your limitations both personally and within the procedures of the school [3-10.2:vi].

There may be a school nurse visiting on occasion or very rarely nowadays a school doctor. Visiting therapists such as occupational, speech and physiotherapists can be very helpful in giving information as to how to cope with pupils with particular needs. There may also be religious or cultural 'dos and don'ts' with some pupils or staff, such as problems with removing certain items of clothing, and you need to be aware of these [3-10.2:v]. The important thing is not to panic, but to make a quick assessment of the situation. Usually your first port of call in any emergency will be to refer to the class teacher, but very quickly in your working day, you may find yourself in a learning area out of sight of such a person. You need to know who can help and how to summon assistance [3-10.2:1]. The emergency aid associations also publish useful manuals about first aid, at work and at home, for adults or children, some of which are available as CD-ROMs. The details can be found on the Red Cross web site (www.redcross.org.uk). While books are useful, nothing can replace actually practising on a course. It is very important to know your own limitations as doing something wrong could further endanger life [3-10.2:vii]. Find out where the trained first-aiders are situated, where people who deal with sick pupils are located, where first aid materials are kept and who has access to them [3-11.3:iv].

You should ensure you can recognise these, check for what to do and what not to do in all the following emergencies [3-10.2:iv]:

a. severe bleeding
b. cardiac arrest
c. shock
d. fainting or loss of consciousness
e. epileptic seizure
f. choking and difficulty with breathing
g. falls – potential and actual fracture
h. burns and scalds
i. poisoning
j. electrocution
k. substance abuse   (LGNTO 2001, Level 2, p. 33)

- Look for danger: you may have to deal with this.
- Remove any danger: only move the casualty if absolutely necessary.
- Assess the casualty: check for consciousness, open the airway, and check for breathing and pulse.
- Get help as soon as you can.

You may be interested to compare the contents of a school first aid kit with one you can buy ready-made; you will probably find fewer items as the rules governing what can be used on other people's children are strict. You should know what to do with a pupil if they have an accident, or if you have an accident.

You should also ensure you know the procedures for dealing with the results of illness as well as the sick pupils. Remember that simple things like reassurance, maintaining some privacy and calmness will help whatever the situation. Afterwards, you may need to clear up vomit, urine, faeces or blood and should find out about protective clothing for yourself like surgical gloves, whether to use sand, sawdust, disinfectant or not and where to locate a site manager or other help in such circumstances. Sickness or accidents to one person can be a health risk to others [3-10.2:4 & viii].

First aid checklist

- Do you know your own limitations in first aid skills?
- Do you know what is expected of you by the school?
- Are there any cultural or religious limitations to your possible actions of which you should be aware?

- Do you know to whom to turn for help?
- Where is the first aid box kept?
- Should you use it?
- What do you do when you have finished using it – whom do you tell about replacing items?
- What would you do if any of the above list happened to you? Or happened to a pupil in your care?

All incidents and accidents should be recorded somewhere in the school, along with the action taken, the time and cause, so be sure you ask about this as well when informing yourself about your appropriate action. The reporting of major incidents can then be dealt with by the appropriate person. You should record incidents in which you are involved; check the requirements for your school [3-10.1:x]. Most schools have notes that can be sent home, signed by someone in authority, to tell parents or carers of incidents in school. It may or may not be your responsibility to inform parents directly; it will depend on the pupil and the nature of the incident [3-11.2:v]. For instance, bumped heads are always considered important, as symptoms of concussion can develop many hours after the incident, so the parents or carers need to be on the lookout for any problem, but the note may need to be signed by a senior member of staff, not you. Some chemicals and medical materials are not allowed in school, and all medicines should be properly secure [3-11.2:viii & 3:vi]. There is more about supporting individual pupils in Chapter 5.

Do not administer medicines or apply ointments or plasters unless you are sure that it is all right. Never use your own creams or lotions on a pupil. Always record your actions.

Equipment, materials and buildings

It is trite, but true, that prevention is better than cure and it is part of your responsibility as a member of staff, particularly one dealing closely with children and young people, to ensure your surroundings are hygienic and safe [3-10.1:2 & 4; 3-11.2]. You will need to get to know the routines for keeping the place tidy and clean [3-10.1:5]. Be firm about school routines, but be careful. It is not your place to criticise or denigrate family customs, but to carry out the customs recommended for your school. For instance, pupils' bags can often be a simple hazard to the passer-by whether in a designated cloakroom area or left lying about a room. Gentle reminders to put them straight can really help, since some pupils appear to have got used to people clearing up for them – that is not your job, but the safety of others is [2-1.1:vi; 3-11.2:1 & 2]. You need to be a good role model yourself where tidiness is concerned.

You may have to visit toilet areas to ensure they are being used properly, and you may need to ensure young pupils wash their hands after using the toilet or before handling food. Make sure you know the appropriate places for you and your pupils to eat or drink in your school. Remember families differ in their standards of tidiness and hygiene at home. Some religious groups do have strict rules about eating particular foods so be careful when commenting on the content of lunch bags [3-11.2:iii]. Some schools may have strict rules about handling soil or animals; most leave it to common sense, that is, wash your hands well after handling either. Fewer schools actually keep animals in schools these days but many still do. Do familiarise yourself with their care in case your particular pupils are interested. The RSPCA has a lot of information about the proper care of animals in schools as well as at home. This includes aquaria and ponds, as well as the more obvious things like mammals [3-10.1:vii]. The World Wildlife Fund has some good information on developing wildlife areas in schools, as do Learning Through Landscapes. Some people can be allergic to animal fur and even caterpillar hairs so *always* ask before bringing any animals to school yourself.

There may be occasions when gender is important, for instance you may have care of a female pupil who begins to menstruate yet has not got any protection with them at school, or even to whom the event comes as a surprise. This can occur as young as eight or nine years of age. Whichever gender you are, make sure you know the school's arrangements for accessing emergency supplies of protective clothing and disposal of soiled materials, and if you are male, identify to whom to go for help should this condition become apparent to you. Some physically disabled girls may need intimate help at this time. Seek clear advice before undertaking this.

Make sure you report any problems with pupils carrying out your hygiene rules or creating unsafe situations, to a teacher or your line manager, as well as any hazard you may find in using any of the school's facilities [3-11.2:6]. The named Health and Safety Officer may need to be informed [3-10.1:vi].

It is your responsibility to ensure that where you work with pupils is safe – you could be asked to take a group in the grounds where there is a pond for instance – and that any tools you work with are used safely. Pupils using tools, equipment and materials should be taught how to use them and how to put them away appropriately and clean after using them [2-1.1:5]. This goes for cutlery at lunch-time and pencil sharpeners as well as craft knives and complicated apparatus. There may be special rules and regulations, even risk assessments associated with particular things, especially if you are helping in science, DT, ICT or art areas. Part of safety routines will be the proper use of tools and equipment, including care and storage. Always read and obey manufacturers' instructions and if in doubt ask for a copy of these. It will be up to you to ensure there is a minimum risk in using such apparatus. All electrical equipment should be used appropriately and safely [3-17.1:3-7]. You may need to be trained to use specialist equipment and that may include specialist safety equipment on lathes or other power tools [2-1.1:2]. If in doubt about the use of any tools or equipment, ask and take note. There is more about health and safety issues in practical subjects in Chapter 10. Clearing up afterwards may also include disposing of materials. Does your school separate waste paper for recycling? Know where and how to dispose of broken glass, chemicals and other possibly toxic materials. Be a good role model in the way you use tools and materials, the way in which you organise your own belongings.

Health and safety procedures also include ensuring security procedures are observed, being alert for strangers and keeping locked areas or equipment that should be away from general use. Schools now contain much expensive equipment such as ICT or laboratory equipment, some of which is highly portable and desirable to thieves. Secondary schools probably have some quite dangerous chemicals and even radioactive materials in various stores. All of us have heard of the, thankfully very rare but devastating, results of aggressive visitors to schools.

A phrase that is often used in schools is 'risk assessment' [3-10.1:2 & v]. This is not necessarily a complicated paper-based task for using dangerous chemicals or machinery but can become part of your everyday thinking. A simple example is teaching children to cross the road safely. You can teach them the Green Cross Code, but as they get older, they will want to cross on their own, where it is not 'safe to cross', say from between parked cars. To do this they need to make a mental assessment of how dangerous the place is, how far they need to go out between the cars after stepping off the kerb to see adequately, whether they have the right footware on to run and so on. We take this kind of assessment for granted, but when in school we do need to be alert for possible dangers, mentally assessing the risk of certain procedures. This does not mean not doing certain procedures which may be interesting or fun, but being sure before you undertake them that you have thought the process through [3-10.1:7]. Some activities need formal risk assessments before they should be undertaken such as visits off site or use of certain chemicals. Risk assessments are routine procedures in science laboratories and DT areas.

- Keep a diary for a week about where you are working with pupils.
- Note any incidents that did happen – what did you do? Could these incidents have been prevented by any action you could have taken?
- Think of all the potential hazards that could have occurred during that week, e.g. spillages, falls, conflicts, injuries, breakages.
- How did you avoid them happening?
- Can you avoid more incidents in future by taking more care?

Dealing with harassment and racist incidents

This is really part of any school policy dealing with equal opportunities, ethos and respect for all individuals, but when such incidents do happen, they can be very personal either to you or the pupils with whom you work closely, and so you are immediately emotionally if not physically involved. Schools have had to produce a race equality policy for 2002/3 which should clearly lay down a framework of positive strategies for ensuring the development of intercultural awareness and education against racism. Various Race Relations Acts (1976 and 2000) and the Code of Practice for Pupils with SEN all give guidance.

The harassment can take the form of physical or verbal attacks, non-cooperation or disrespect and other incidents such as use of certain language printed on clothing, badges or posters, or other more subtle incidents.

It is important that you know the key actions to take following any such incidents:

- Take immediate and appropriate action to deal with the incident.
- Deal with it as objectively as possible, not attacking the perpetrator in a personal manner – what is done is wrong, not the person doing it.
- Notify the person indicated in the policy and complete any required documents.
- Provide support for the victim, expressing your concern.
- A senior member of staff may have to inform and deal with parents of pupils involved, either as victims or perpetrators.
- Discuss the matter with your line manager as to who should counsel and discuss the problem with the perpetrator, explaining why the actions are not to be tolerated.

As in all cases of health and safety, prevention is better than having to deal with the incident and so following the positive policies and ethos of the school will really help. Teachers can include discussion of such matters in their curriculum planning or circle times. Also remember that the perpetrator can see ignoring such incidents as condoning them. If any incident is aimed at you personally, seek advice from your line manager in dealing with it.

Using the office – other staff and equipment

It may be tempting to use the school facilities liberally to support your own work, but time and materials all cost money and schools are usually very careful about their budgets. Do ensure you know if and when you can use the telephone, whether on school or personal business, and if there is a kitty to which you should contribute when doing so. The school administrative staff are there to help all staff with clerical work, but will have their priorities and procedures too. Ask your line manager before asking for help with typing or photocopying, and even if you are doing the photocopying, ensure you know the procedures for obtaining more paper or ink. *Never* take the last packet without telling someone you have done so or replenishing the supply if you know how. The next person to use the machine is sure to be in a hurry.

If you have a personal question about salary payment or similar, find out when is a good time to talk to the finance officer or bursar. If you want to speak to a senior member of staff or the head, it is usually wise to make an appointment, even if informally. Make sure that any written communication you have regarding pupils is legible, accurate, up to date and kept in a secure place [2-1.2:3].

If you want to borrow any school equipment or bring in some of your own, such as a tape recorder or laptop, make sure you ask about insurance as well as getting permission for such a thing. Ensure your car is insured to carry passengers for business purposes before you offer to ferry anyone anywhere.

Communication

Communication is the lifeblood of an organisation, it is what connects everybody together so that the organisation can function. It operates two ways [2-4.1:iii]. You must communicate with your pupils and class teachers, but also your line manager, mentor, curriculum managers or coordinators, union representatives, administrative and caretaking staff – all those with whom you may come into contact. You may not like some of them as people, but you must not show this at work. Always remain pleasant and calm – confrontation rarely achieves the best results and conflict always has to be resolved by some sort of compromise in the end. Respond to any consultations promptly, bring necessary things to the appropriate person's attention – things that may be concerning you such as the condition of toilets or a shortage of recording tapes [2-1.1:8; 2-4.1:iv].

If you are given written guidance read it, read memos and newsletters, notices and handouts. File them, even if they seem irrelevant, and revise the filing every so often to throw out outdated materials. Do not issue documents or post messages on boards unless you are sure it is appropriate to do so. Messages can be verbal – if you have a poor memory, then make a note, keep a small jotter in your pocket along with a pencil or biro. Messages can also be non-verbal so particularly when new to an organisation, watch out for body language. You may be sitting on the chair in the staffroom that only certain people ever sit on by tradition. Be sensitive to looks or gestures. Pupils can communicate non-verbally too [2-4.1].

Ensure that any photocopying you do falls within the copyright laws. Most schools display a copy of these by the side of the machine, and indicate where records of numbers of copies should be recorded of extracts of published items if this is relevant.

It is your responsibility to read any policies, guidance or guidelines given to you and to follow what is stated in them. If you do not agree with any of the contents then ask your line manager how such advice came about and what the procedures are for consultation in the school. Then use the proper routes to get things changed if it is important to you. Some documents will be useful to get general information on the way the school works such as the prospectus, the parental newsletters and the Annual Report to Parents. Attending meetings is also part of your responsibility. This may cause a problem with your child care facilities if the meeting is arranged after pupil contact hours, and you may have to negotiate to be paid for such attendance. These meetings may be of any of the teams to which you belong, planning meetings with a teacher or meetings with specialists or for your appraisal. These are all necessary to the smooth running of any organisation. Paper messages will not substitute for verbal discussions or face-to-face working [2-4.1:iv]. Do attend the Annual Meeting held by the governors, although this would probably be considered to be done in your own time for all the staff.

Confidentiality

As a member of staff, a professional (and this should apply to volunteers as well), you should maintain confidentiality about all that you see or hear or read while you are in school. Children may behave differently at school compared with other situations and environments. For instance, you may have known them previously in a pre-school setting, or know them in a social context, or see them with their parents. Teachers may comment on children's progress. You may wish the child received more attention at home, or was kept away from another child, but that cannot be said outside the professional dialogue with staff in the school. Parents do approach TAs about their children, thinking either they are less busy than teachers, or even that they are a softer touch, or they know you anyway. It can be difficult not to relay gossip to a friend, when you are dying to tell someone.

If you are dealing with written records about any pupil or person in the organisation, keep the highest standards of confidentiality. There are likely to be procedures for access to such records, and recognised places for keeping them. Make sure you know what these are [2-1.2:5 & iii; 2-4.1:6].

The learning environment

The surroundings in which learning takes place influence the quality of the learning [2-1.1]. You know yourself that having things where you know where you can find them – materials or tools – makes a job easier or not. Having the right lighting or a comfortable chair at the correct height makes a difference to how long you can persist at a task. Sharp tools are usually safer than blunt ones. A jigsaw with lost pieces is useless, blunt pencils will not produce good hand-writing, paper with curled edges does not encourage good presentation. A welcoming room or building encourages its use.

You are responsible for all the equipment or materials you use, and should provide a role model on your use of them. You will need to find out where items are kept that you will be using and how to use them properly [2-1.1:3,4]. This will include knowing about storage facilities [2-1.1:v], and what to do if you or a pupil you are with breaks or spills anything, and how to dispose of waste of any kind [3-10.1:6 & viii]. This goes for pencils, paper and scissors as well as televisions, audio or computer equipment, scientific equipment or chemicals, tools, toys and books. Check *before* a lesson that you have correct and sufficient materials for a task, never leave your pupils to go to get something, particularly if they are young and away from their class base. The teacher should give you a copy of his or her planning or enable you to have access to it so that you can see what you will need, and should be able to answer any queries you have. Again communication before the lesson about any such queries should be the norm.

Give time towards the end of any task to clear up, clean or return equipment, check the equipment and leave the work station tidy for its next user [2-1.1:6,7]. Even reception class children can wash paint pots, you do not have to do it for them. If you are concerned about the way in which pupils handle materials, tools or equipment, if they are wasteful or destructive, then inform the class teacher. Your joint care of such items should become part of a routine way of working.

It may be part of your job description to care particularly for some items in school – as a librarian or technician, or attached to a particular classroom or area of the building. Where possible, with permission, involve the pupils in such a task. You may be asked to stock check certain areas regularly such as art materials, or regularly tape record broadcast programmes. Be as tidy and organised as possible so that others can access your system if you are away or ill. If the equipment has a specific use, make sure you know how to use it properly and safely, and how it is cared for. You may need to consult specific subject teachers for help in this. The school grounds will also have specific uses, and maintenance procedures, so check before gaily digging a flowerbed for worms, or picking samples of leaves [2-1.1:i, ii].

Records

Pupils' and staff records will be kept under lock and key somewhere centrally usually, although some of the running records will be in the pupils' classrooms. You must find out the systems and procedures for your school, and what your roles and responsibilities are within those [2-1.2:i & ii]. Maintain their safe and secure storage at all times, and do not leave important documents on the photocopier. It is easily done. Another trap is the use of paperclips. Single sheets of paper can easily get attached to the wrong set of documents with these helpful things.

The safe storage of data also applies to matters kept on computers. All material kept on adults or pupils on computer hard or floppy disks is subject to the Data Protection Act which means that it all must be kept securely, and the subject of the item stored should have access to what is being stored. If you are asked to enter data into pupils' records on a database, ensure you know the procedures your school adopts to conform with this Act [2-1.2:iv]. In principle only the minimum personal information necessary is stored, which should be as accurate as possible and only held for as long as necessary. Individuals have a right to see what is stored about them except in very limited circumstances where 'access would prejudice the prevention or detection of crime' (DOH, HO and DfEE 1999: 115). Security measures do not just include the physical security of the equipment but the existence of appropriate levels of staff access. Never divulge passwords to office equipment unless requested to by the senior member of staff responsible for the recording systems.

The School Development Plan (SDP)

One major vehicle of management and communication within a school with which you should familiarise yourself is a School Development (or Improvement) Plan (SDP or SIP). This is the business plan of the organisation and should cover all the areas of operation of the school including the teaching assistants. This plan is produced annually, usually after a review of the previous one and frequently after consultation with all the people concerned in the plan. Sometimes a major review of the plan is undertaken – after an inspection or sometimes just triennially. These are often lengthy and rather unwieldy documents and you will not need to read all of it. There will always be a reference copy available in schools and sometimes major parts of it are displayed in a prominent place such as the foyer or the staffroom and items highlighted as they are achieved. There is usually a summary version for circulation. This may be in the Annual Report to Parents. It is your responsibility as an employee to make sure you know about the bits that may affect you. Look under the staffing section, or special needs or the curriculum areas with which you are associated. The development of ICT or behaviour management strategies may affect your work, proposals for changes to the fabric of the building may impinge upon your effectiveness. It is also your responsibility to respond if consulted in the review process [2-4.1:iv]. There should be a support staff member of the governing body somewhere, who will be representing you on the governing body. From September 2003, governing bodies will not have to make specific provision for a member of the support staff to be a governor – all governing bodies will have 'staff' governors. This category will include teaching and support staff. Identify them and make any concerns you have known to them. They can then take this to the governors, who have to approve the plan annually.

Figure 4.1 is a real example from an SDP for you to see the kind of things that may be written.

Dimension 8 People Management

With regard to this dimension, we wish to maintain our Investors in People status and build upon this achievement. We also wish to look closely at how the team structure might be developed in order for it to contribute effectively to the standards raising agenda.

Objectives/ Target	Success criteria – expected standards to be reached	Action to be taken	Time scale/ completion date	Person responsible – lead, monitor, report	Costs – time, training, finance and resources	Monitoring of target (data to be used)	Evaluation process – method of assessing impact – progress check
To review the team structure in terms of its contribution to raising standards throughout the school	An effective team structure is in place with a clear brief to contribute to the raising and maintaining of standards throughout the school	Senior management team to consider the current team system and the contribution it makes to school improvement. Recommendations to be drawn up and submitted to governors	By April 2002	HT and senior management team	Time for discussion and decision making	Outcomes of proposed development on pupils' learning. Do minutes of team meetings indicate agenda of standards raising? Is there evidence that teams are making a difference to the education provided in the school?	HT and Personnel Committee to monitor
To review our staff development procedures with a view to maintaining our IiP status	Staff development enhanced and IiP status retained	Use new IiP standards to review current practice and make changes accordingly	By Summer 2002	HT, staff development manager	Time and eventual costs of IiP review	Staff development meets IiP standards	HT, senior management team and Personnel Committee
To ensure that the performance management procedures are operating effectively	Performance management policy fully implemented for this round and in the future	HT and senior management team to manage this process in line with policy	Ongoing	Senior management team	Time and release costs – £2000 per year	Performance management helping to focus minds on school improvement	HT and senior managers to consult staff re effectiveness of this process
To continue to develop the development portfolios for support staff	Support staff have opportunities for development and professional dialogue	DHT to take leading role in organising the development portfolio meetings	Ongoing	DHT	Time – release costs for DHT	Do LSAs feel supported and valued?	HT to monitor

Figure 4.1 Page 30 from a School Development Plan relating to people management   © Source: Maldon Primary School, Essex

50

5 The education, care and support of pupils

Schools are for educating pupils, they are not children's homes or day care centres. The staff are there first and foremost to enable the pupils to learn. In doing this the staff themselves are always learning and so the whole school is a learning institution. However, as staff are also *in loco parentis*, they do have a duty of care while the pupils are present, and while learners need a challenge, unhappy or uncomfortable people do not learn as well as happy, healthy, motivated ones. Therefore staff need to ensure that the learning environment is healthy – both hygienic and safe, as well as having the right atmosphere or climate to foster good relationships between all who work there.

General health

It was pointed out in Chapter 2 that you need to take care of your own health, but you also need to be alert to changes in your pupils.

> Teachers and other school staff have a common law duty to act as any proud parent would to make sure that pupils are healthy and safe on school premises and this might in exceptional circumstances, extend to administering medicine and/or taking action in an emergency.
>
> (DfEE 1996: 3)

There will be school policies in place for all health, hygiene and medical matters. You must make sure you have a copy of all the relevant ones and that you have read them, understand them and follow the guidelines set out in them [3-11.2:i & vii]. Sick children or adults will not work well, and may be infectious to other pupils. If you see anything that concerns you, always tell the class teacher [3-11.3:3]. Sometimes children come to school with minor ailments, and you need to be able to deal with these, such as a heavy cold. It is sometimes useful, particularly with small children in winter, to equip yourself with a box of tissues or a soft toilet roll to deal with runny noses. Children do not need to be off school for a cold, but you can help prevent its spread to others. Dispose of the used materials properly. A polythene bag with you could contain the used material which could then go to an incinerator or adult toilet. Ask for advice on procedures like this.

Always reassure ill pupils, and comfort unhappy ones, but only verbally unless they seek physical comfort from you [2-2.1:5]. Comforting must be done in an appropriate manner and place. A returned hug in a public place from a small child missing a parent is one thing, but the same action in a quiet corner can be misconstrued [3-11.3:5]. Younger children need more physical support than older ones and are less likely to be able to tell you what is wrong if they are miserable. Be sure to read the section on child protection below. You may need to summon help [3-10.2:ii]. Some schools have a simple card communication system where staff have access to the cards which are sent in an emergency to the office. Depending on the colour of the card, the office alert the appropriate support. It could be red for a fight, green for illness and yellow for an accident, for instance. Enquire whether you are able to use such a system in your school. It may be important to help pupils not directly involved in an incident, who can suffer shock particularly if the incident is severe. This is the kind of role you can play if you have to summon expert help: you will be able to support the onlookers. This may just be reassurance or removing them from the incident site [3-10.2:2, 3, 4 & ix].

You need to be able to recognise if a pupil you are working with is just 'under the weather' or is really feeling ill [3-11.3:1 & i]. The important thing is to get to know the pupils with whom you are working closely, what is their normal range of behaviour and appearance, then you will recognise significant changes should they occur. As you are likely to be working more closely with the pupils than any other member of staff, you may be the first to notice [3-10.2.i; 3-11.2:3].

The sort of things you may notice are:

- changes in facial colour – becoming very red or pale, becoming very hot or cold, becoming clammy or shivering – fever usually means some kind of infection;
- changes in behaviour like not wanting to go out at break-time when they usually want to be first out;
- general distress;
- reduced concentration, which can even be to the point of falling asleep at their desk;
- scratching more than usual – ask about the school policy regarding head lice – you should not examine a head unless it is appropriate in your school;
- complaining of pain which persists, particularly if they are not easily distracted from mentioning it, including headaches and stomach pain;
- rashes – these can develop rapidly and may be associated with fever in the case of infection or could be an allergic reaction;
- coughing and sneezing excessively;
- diarrhoea or vomiting – these you will have to deal with as emergencies [3-11.3:1].

You should not try to diagnose from these conditions, although always note any unusual circumstances that you see or the pupil mentions. They may talk of strange tasting food, or parties, circumstances changing at home, visitors to home or recent holidays. Your role is to recognise the changes and report them appropriately, unless there is an emergency to deal with. You will soon recognise the difference between the pupils who want a brief spell in the sick room or a bit more attention, and the threat of 'I am going to be sick' which needs immediate action. Make sure you know where or to whom to send sick pupils, and to whom to report the symptoms you have noticed. You may even need to summon help rather than leave a sick pupil [3.11.3:4].

Remember too, changes in mental and emotional state can also occur, particularly if something traumatic or dramatic has happened at home which can show itself in unhappiness, mood swings, lack of concentration and attention-seeking or withdrawal from activities [3-11.3:6 & ii]. Some cultures and religions do have different ways of dealing with illness, so if in doubt, ask [3-11.3:ii]. The age of the pupil will affect how well they can tell you what is wrong; once you know the pupil well you will be able to tell how reliable any information from them might be and the circumstances of the incident. Some pupils can fake illness if they do not like sports or the weather is inclement. There may be changes in patterns of behaviour. A small child who has always come to chat stands alone, or a teenager usually friendly is moody or withdrawn, or a usually quiet but confident pupil follows you around. It could be just growing up, the hormones of puberty taking over, or it could signify something more significant. Either way, you need mentally to register the changes, keep an eye on the pupil over a period of time and if really concerned talk to the pupil's teacher or tutor. Such changes could signify problems at home, even abuse of some kind, self-inflicted substance abuse, or bullying within or outside the school [2-2.1:x; 3-1.1:ix]. If the pupil will talk to you follow the guidelines set out below regarding child protection – never promise confidentiality, always tell someone of the conversation and make a simple record of it.

Many TAs are appointed to help a child with special learning or physical needs [3-11.3:2]. You must ensure you know the full extent of your role and responsibilities with any pupil, and all the appropriate ways to support them, and whether there are particular changes or signs peculiar to them of which you should be aware [2-2.1:i]. For instance, sometimes pupils are on particular medication which has certain specified effects, or they may need to be given that medication at a particular time. You should familiarise yourself with any particular needs of pupils with whom you may come into contact. If these details are not readily available in the staffroom, check with your line manager. Also, there may be pupils with whom you are not directly coming in contact, but who do have specific conditions of which you should be aware. Most schools now ensure all staff know of pupils with allergies such as peanut or bee sting allergy, or the existence of pupils with diabetes, epilepsy or other disorders. These conditions could have crises with which you may need to deal appropriately. Each individual will have their own medication or procedures for dealing with any incidents.

One condition that has become more common is asthma; approximately one pupil in four will have some kind of allergic or asthmatic condition, some much worse than others, some just manifesting as hay fever in the summer or a sensitivity to certain drugs. You should check at some early point whether you will be working with pupils who suffer from asthma, where they keep their inhalers and how they are used. Usually schools have information from the Asthma Association which you can read.

- Ask your line manager for the four most common ailments of pupils within the school.
- See what more you can find out about these ailments.
- Find out whether these ailments are treated the same way in all countries.
- Does your school have any pupils from the countries where customs are different?
- Find out more about any conditions that apply to pupils you are working with closely.
- Does the school have any written guidelines in any of these areas?
- Do you have a copy?

Whatever the problem, make sure you know where and when to seek help, what kind of written records are needed and to whom you should report any concerns, including whether you contact parents directly or notify someone else to do this [3-10.2:6 & x; 3-11.3:7 & iii].

Health education [3-11.2:vi]

The school will also have a policy to do with health education of the pupils. It is usually located in what is colloquially called PSHE – personal, social and health education. This will cover areas such as sex education, how to help pupils with personal hygiene, diet and exercise, but also emotional and mental health. It will deal with matters like self-esteem, its importance and how to promote it, bullying and coping with it, whether the school has access to people with counselling skills. While you will not be directly responsible necessarily for teaching pupils in any of these areas, your relationships with them are very important in enabling them to grow into mature, self-confident adults. A healthy school is not only hygienic and safe physically but a welcoming and secure place with good relationships between all who work there. Your example to the pupils is important. You can show by the way you talk to colleagues or pupils, by your tone of voice, what can be expected. The way you listen, or are prepared to follow up problems, get help. Even remembering names shows that you care and are prepared to bother about others. If you are willing to assist with preparation of resources for teachers or get someone a cup of tea when they are fed up or overstretched, it shows you can think about them and do something practical to assist [3-11.2:1, 2 & ii]. If all staff had such an attitude, the school would be a good place to work and pupils would soon recognise the place as a good place to learn.

It is highly likely that you will be asked questions by pupils [3-11.2:4], as they get to know you and you work in close proximity to a small group or individuals. Note that primary schools only have to have a sex education policy, that policy does not have to ensure sex education is done by the school; it may indicate that it should be done at home.

Find out

- Should you listen to the exploits of the teenagers without comment, such as:
  - smoking on the school premises?
  - substance abuse?
  - getting drunk at the weekend?
  - declaring their sexual habits or preferences or that they are pregnant?
- What do you do if you are told of incidents of bullying, or disastrous friend-ships?
- Can you talk about HIV and Aids if they ask the questions?
- What should you do if they show you pornography?
- Should you comment on a pupil's diet or exercise level to them even if they seem excessively thin or obese?
- Whom do you tell if they are so upset about something it is affecting the way they behave?
- Simple ways to boost pupils' self-esteem.

There are various books such as Fox (2001: 19–31) and Hook and Vass (2000: 22–38) which have some really useful things to say about promoting self-esteem in pupils. Some suggestions are as follows:

- Talk to everyone the same way, regardless of gender, race or background.
- Address pupils by their preferred name.
- Use positive comments: 'thank you for walking', 'well done for being quiet', including written comments if you can: 'well read today', 'I liked the story'.
- Use praise appropriately, not indiscriminately.
- Treat boys and girls equally, whether for tasks or treats or even lining up.
- Provide a good role model in gender, culture and disability, both in reality and when finding examples in teaching materials such as books and magazines.
- Use rewards, praise and congratulation systems for work, including showing it to other staff.
- Catch them being good or working hard and tell them.
- Set small achievable targets and congratulate them on achieving them.
- Have reward systems for behaviour – telling the teachers about the good as well as the troublesome.
- Value work by ensuring it is taken care of, and presented well, both by you and the pupil.
- Encourage independence appropriate to age and maturity.
- Enable and encourage peer tutoring.
- Use humour carefully.
- Encourage children to value their own performance.
- Listen to the views of pupils and act on them where possible.
- Avoid being patronising or sarcastic as pupils recognise both.

Can you add to this?   (Watkinson 2002: 38)

Settling pupils

One area where you are likely to be involved, particularly if you are working with children in the early years class, sometimes called the reception class, or with Year 7s in a secondary school (Year 5s or 9s if your area has a middle school system) is with pupils who are very new to the school [3-11.1]. The school is likely to have well thought out procedures, some of which will have taken place before you meet them. The teachers may have visited their previous school or playgroup, or even their homes, and pupils are most likely to have had at least one visit to the school before their first 'real' day. You need to find out what these procedures are and may even accompany members of the teaching staff on their visits [3-11.1:ii].

Remember

- How you felt when you started school.
- How you felt when you transferred schools.
- How you felt when you started this new job.
- How you felt if you went to a new school if you moved house as a child.
- What helped you to settle?
- Who helped you to settle?
- How long did it take?
- So – what can you do to help newcomers to your school?

All sorts of things affect a child's ability to settle in a new environment [3-11.1:iii]. If things are troubling them at home – say their parents have broken up, which necessitated the house move – it is not just the new school that is troubling them, but new neighbours *and* missing one of their parents. Making new friends can be a problem when changing schools. They may have come from another country with different customs. They may not speak our language. They may have had a period away from the school, while a parent serves with the armed services or during a return visit to their native land. The sort of thing to look out for is a child who is not mixing with others at break times, one who cries without apparently being hurt or one who is clinging on to you, a pupil of any age who cannot follow instructions or get on with their work, but does not appear to have learning problems. A young child may wet themselves, afraid to ask for the toilet, or fall asleep because they are not sleeping well at night, worried about their new school. Small children anxious at starting school are even likely to run away unless the school has made proper arrangements for the first few days. Older pupils attending the new large secondary school after their relatively cosy, probably much smaller primary school will feel very lost. They will have to carry their bags around to various classrooms instead of having a classroom and a few well-known teachers for most subjects. Generally, an unsettled child will be fearful and tearful, but such feelings could manifest themselves in angry or even aggressive behaviour as the child is cross at being put in this strange situation

[3-11.1.iv]. Pupils with learning problems, a disability or with little ability to communicate either because of home language being different or through speech problems may have a higher risk of unease with new situations, as they find it more difficult to understand what is happening. But beware of misinterpreting the reasons for difficult behaviour. Always talk matters through with the teacher if you have concerns, and respond as he or she directs [3-11.1:4 & 5].

As a TA, you can be invaluable in settling pupils in. It may be an idea to negotiate with the teachers for you just to be available for this task at the beginning of a new school year. In this way the pupils will get down to the school work much more quickly and satisfactorily. It may even be important to change your timetable for a couple of weeks to spend more time at the beginnings and ends of days ensuring the new ones know where they are going and get there happily. The teacher may ask you to liaise directly with the parents and stagger entry and exit times for the new pupils. In this way an easier transition can take place, especially if a larger number are starting together. Changing classrooms or teachers can unsettle pupils. A constant change of teacher when supply teachers are standing in for a teacher on sick leave can also be a problem. In these situations you may be the one constant person in their school lives. Do ensure you talk to the class teacher if you continue to notice signs of distress after a week or so, or to a more senior teacher if the class teacher's absence is the problem. Talk any problems through with the class teacher [3-11.1:5].

Strategies that may help to settle pupils [3-11.1:1 & i]

- Be warm and welcoming.
- Learn to recognise distressed pupils.
- Learn their names as soon as possible.
- Make sure they know the name of their class teacher or tutor and encourage the other pupils with you to befriend and help the newcomer.
- Make sure they know where they are going round the building, where their next classroom is, where their cloakroom and the toilets are and to whom they can go if they are worried.
- Smile at them when you see them in the building but are not directly working with them.
- Allow them to talk about their previous school or playschool.
- Allow them to work a little more slowly at first.
- Have patience, listen and possibly talk about your own experiences if appropriate.
- Keep to classroom routines and where possible the layout.
- Make sure you know whether they have special educational needs or speak a different language.
- Try wording your sentences more simply if that is a problem.
- Try to learn a few words of their language, as they begin to learn our words – their words for mum and dad, for home and toilet, bag, book and table would do for a start.

- Carry the tissue box with you in case of tears.
- Ensure you tell their class teacher or tutor if they have problems after the first week [3-11.1:1, 2, 3 & i].

Child protection

It is essential to know about this, although it is a sensitive area [2-2.1:ix; 3-10.1:iv; 3-11.3:vii]. Some of you may have had close personal involvement with family or friends where problems have arisen, or feel that these matters are better not dealt with until an incident arises. You will all have been checked by the police through the Criminal Records Bureau before you took up post. However, there are a couple of things that, as a member of staff likely to come into close physical and pastoral contact with pupils, you need to be aware of. It is hoped that all schools these days have written policies in this area and make sure all staff are trained together, but it does not always happen. If it does not happen in your school, then suggest it.

There are legal and organisational requirements and implications for you when you work with other people's children [3-11.2:ix]. Teachers and other school staff act *in loco parentis*. The Children Act applies to schools as well as the general population. The school policy should lay out clear guidelines for *all* staff on what to do if there is a suspicion of abuse and on how to prevent allegations against staff themselves. There should be a designated Child Protection person whose name is known by all staff, who is trained in what to do and where to go if help is needed.

There are two main areas of sensitivity, one in recognising the signs of abuse and the other in behaving appropriately as a member of staff. All staff should be aware of the possible signs of abuse (see Table 5.1), which are not always physical. It can also be mental, emotional or the result of neglect. While some of these signs can be listed, they must be considered only indicators. All sorts of personal or family events can cause changes in behaviour. The important thing is to tell someone senior to yourself of your concern, as patterns may emerge when several people's evidence is collated, or several different signs appear on or with the same pupil [3-1.1:ix].

Table 5. 1 Signs and symptoms of abuse

Possible signs of physical abuse

- Unexplained injuries or burns, particularly if they are recurrent
- Refusal to discuss injuries
- Improbable explanations for injuries
- Untreated injuries or lingering illness not attended to
- Admission of punishment which appears excessive
- Shrinking from physical contact
- Fear of returning home or of parents being contacted
- Fear of undressing
- Fear of medical help
- Aggression/bullying

- Over-compliant behaviour or a 'watchful attitude'
- Running away
- Significant changes in behaviour without explanation
- Deterioration in work
- Unexplained pattern of absences which may serve to hide bruises or other physical injuries

Possible signs of emotional abuse

- Continual self-deprecation
- Fear of new situations
- Inappropriate emotional responses to painful situations
- Self-harm or mutilation
- Compulsive stealing/scrounging
- Drug/solvent abuse
- 'Neurotic' behaviour – obsessive rocking, thumb-sucking and so on
- Air of detachment – 'don't care' attitude
- Social isolation – does not join in and has few friends
- Desperate attention-seeking behaviour
- Eating problems, including overeating and lack of appetite
- Depression, withdrawal

Possible signs of neglect

- Constant hunger
- Poor personal hygiene
- Inappropriate clothing
- Frequent lateness or non-attendance at school
- Untreated medical problems
- Low self-esteem
- Poor social relationships
- Compulsive stealing or scrounging
- Constant tiredness

Possible signs of sexual abuse

- Bruises, scratches, burns or bite marks on the body
- Scratches, abrasions or persistent infections in the anal or genital regions
- Pregnancy – particularly in the case of young adolescents who are evasive concerning the identity of the father
- Sexual awareness inappropriate to the child's age – shown, for example, in drawings, vocabulary, games and so on
- Frequent public masturbation
- Attempts to teach other children about sexual activity
- Refusing to stay with certain people or go to certain places
- Aggressiveness, anger, anxiety, tearfulness
- Withdrawal from friends

Possible signs in older children

- Promiscuity, prostitution, provocative sexual behaviour
- Self-injury, self-destructive behaviour, suicide attempts
- Eating disorders
- Tiredness, lethargy, listlessness
- Over-compliant behaviour
- Sleep disturbances
- Unexplained gifts of money
- Depression
- Changes in behaviour

Source: Schonveld 1995: 18–19

Do not use this list as being definitive: you need proper training from the LEA Child Protection Officer or whoever does it in your area. All children can have bruises from accidents or playing roughly. It is the type of bruise and where it is on the body that can be important. Do not be obsessive or inquisitive, but just be vigilant, for instance when children change for PE or are talking informally.

Revealing

A child may reveal to you what has happened to them. You are particularly well placed for children to feel secure with you. You will work in small groups or with individual pupils for periods of time and build up friendly relations. No school staff are trained to deal with children or families in detail in child protection matters but you all have a responsibility to recognise and report to people who are. You should not question a child in these circumstances as you may ask leading questions. You should never promise not to tell anyone. Listen carefully, sensitively, caringly, inwardly note what they say and then tell the named designated member of staff as soon as possible. Make a short written record afterwards, date it and give it to this named member of staff. It is that person's responsibility to deal with it by informing Social Services or the police, who do have trained personnel for helping the children and their families and any matters that arise.

It is difficult, because you make assumptions or have memories which could prevent you from listening properly, but it is a responsibility that you take on when working in a school. If you have any doubts about what you have heard or seen, and these incidents are rarely clear cut, discuss what you have seen or heard with the class teacher, your teacher mentor, the designated teacher or the head. If you are involved further, be guided by the named person in the school. These people will understand about case conferences, child protection registers, and agencies who can support vulnerable children and their families. Of course, you maintain confidentiality with the staff concerned, in all these proceedings.

The other area where you can be involved in these issues is when you are dealing with children in intimate situations. Again this often happens when TAs have been appointed to deal with pupils with physical disabilities, or very young children who have toileting accidents. Usually the parents know what the policy is as well, whether school staff can clean children up after toilet accidents or change underclothes. TAs are sometimes asked to work in pairs when these events occur. Always comfort unhappy children, but do it in public not privately. Pupils need sometimes to see school as a haven, place of safety and security which they may not otherwise have, but do not put yourself into a situation that could lead to unjustified accusation. Always be aware of, and respond to, troubled children, but recognise how to do this appropriately. Do not single them out for attention; it is better for them to come to you.

Contact

Another aspect of this can be when dealing with difficult pupils. Again, you may have been appointed just for this purpose. The proper procedures cannot be taught to you in a book. Touching pupils, let alone restraining pupils, can get you into difficulties with parents and even the law. The pupils concerned are usually particularly volatile, liable to act up, or react unnecessarily to being told how to behave. So do make sure you know the school policy on restraint, and if possible get appropriate training in this area. You should not be in a difficult position with a pupil swearing in your face, being aggressive or dangerous to others in your early days in the school. Make sure you talk quickly to your line manager and sort out who does what. Most LEAs have people who will be specialists in this area who can help.

In all these health and safety issues it is vital that you know the policies and procedures that exist for your school. Some of these may be based on national guidance. They may seem irksome but they are written to protect the pupils and you. Ensure you know about what liaison there is with parents over various incidents, what records the school requires to be kept and maintain confidentiality appropriately at all times [3-11.3:v, vi, ix].

Implications for your role

Dealing with other people's children can leave you in a vulnerable position, open to allegations of abuse against you, sometimes made by quite small children. Such is the publicity given to child protection matters these days, and the angry, emotional responses by some people to any suspicion of abuse, that children in households where such matters are discussed in this manner may see an opportunity for some meddling or an opportunity for attention. In order to prevent such false allegations, you are advised to ensure that you do not put yourself in a position where it is only the pupil's word against yours. Follow strictly any guidance given to you by the school. Try to deal with toileting accidents with a colleague, do not stay alone in classrooms with only one or two pupils late in the day, do not put a child on your lap, particularly if you are male, unless it is essential to their well-being and you are in an open situation. Discuss this issue with your mentor at an early stage.

Development and maturity

While you do not need a detailed understanding of how pupils develop in all their facets at Level 2, some recognition of this is essential. However well the curriculum is 'delivered', pupils are not empty vessels to be filled up. Some knowledge of facts is important but with ever-increasing access to sources of facts in books or electronic format, sheer accumulation of facts is less crucial than knowing how to access them. The pace of change also means that facts change. Understanding is important, as are attitudes to learning and the skills to use the facts.

We are made up of a physical body, with genetically determined characteristics. As soon as we are conceived, the environment in which we grow will affect how we develop, including how we learn. Diet, experiences, exposure to climate and culture will all affect our development.

Get out your family photograph album.

Select ten photographs of yourself over your life from birth to the present day, at as even intervals as you can.

What changes have taken place? Look at each photo and note:

- How much you grew physically
- Family changes
- Changes in friends
- Places you have lived in
- Places you went to learn
- Places you visited

You will also have developed physically, socially, emotionally, culturally and spiritually. Sometimes the physical growth was fast and sometimes not. Some periods like puberty were emotionally insecure. Age made a difference as to how you coped with changes, but gender also affected what you were able to do. Learning develops in just such an erratic way, affected by inherited characteristics but also affected by experiences, age, gender, culture and environment. Some people are naturally talented in one area, artistically, musically, or in sport or mathematics, learning seems to come easily to them in that area. Others are good at forming friendships and some are natural leaders, their personality affecting their attitudes. Attitudes to learning are important, and can in turn be affected by the need to learn, motivation, interest and the way you are helped or challenged [2-3.2:iv].

All pupils have educational needs and it will be your job to assist in that process, supporting the processes of learning and the teacher in his or her aims for them. However, all pupils, all children, all adults are different in the way they learn and their need for support. The more you can observe and learn yourself about these differences, the better you will be at supporting the pupils. Despite these differences, it makes sense also to look at similarities, to teach together those whose needs are similar. The easiest way to do this is to put pupils in age groups, as developmental stages roughly come together. Then schools sometimes ability set within these age groups and you may well have a group of similar learners to work with. However, pupils with different ability often help each other, so teachers have to be flexible.

Within the broad age groups there will be pupils with particular needs, usually referred to as having special educational needs (SEN). They may have problems in any or several of the areas of development. Sometimes they have physical disabilities which mean access to the learning environment is difficult, or they may have delayed or damaged physical growth of their brain which means their very learning capability is slower than others. Problems at home can influence how they learn at school. Pupils often find learning hard during puberty when their emotions are in turmoil, the hormones seeming more in control than the brain [2-3.2:v]. Chapter 6 deals with this area of providing for differences yet recognising similarities.

Learning

Small children learn through play as their language and co-ordination matures. They need to touch and smell, hear and see things to understand. They can then tackle things like learning to read and write much more quickly. Older children can conceptualise mentally more and so can learn more through people telling them things, or reading about them. In some cultures being male or female means not undertaking some activities. Unhappy or starving children will have more problems learning than well-fed, secure ones. Learning is also cumulative, it needs previous experiences on which to build. It also needs practice, as any musician will tell you.

Think of a recent learning experience since you became an adult.

- Why did you have to do this thing?
- What steps did you make to start?
- What and who helped you while you did it?
- What or who hindered you while you did it?
- How did it finish – or is it continuing?

Make a list of the factors that affected your learning process.

Then make a list of factors that could affect the pupils with whom you are working most closely.

Share this with your mentor.

By remembering how you learn and what helps you, you will become more sensitive to how the pupils with whom you work learn. Doing some recorded observations of pupils which you share with your mentor is a useful way of developing your own understanding of how children learn. Pages 39 to 43 of the book *Assisting learning and supporting teaching* (Watkinson 2002) have some ways of doing such observations. A few ideas follow.

Observation techniques

With the knowledge and help of your class teacher or mentor, select a pupil in the class who has learning problems and watch them for half a minute every five minutes in half an hour. Make notes.

- What do they do?
- What do they say?

Discuss what you saw with the teacher.

- What factors are affecting that pupil's learning process?
- What more could have been done during that time to assist the learning process?

- What factors are out of the school's control but help you understand what happens to that pupil?
- Are there any areas about which you can seek more information?

Dispose of your notes appropriately.

It is important to ensure you know what your role and responsibilities are regarding learning with all the pupils with whom you will be working. [2-3.1:iii]. There are various strategies that can help you support pupils to facilitate their learning. Types of support might be:

a. prompting shy or reticent pupils
b. translating or explaining words and phrases used by the teacher
c. reminding pupils of teaching points made by the teacher
d. modelling correct use of language and vocabulary
e. ensuring that pupils understand and follow the teacher's instructions
f. providing a supportive audience
g. helping pupils to use resources relevant to the learning activity
h. facilitating discussions and interactions   (LGNTO 2001, Level 2, p. 22)

- Find out what interests them.
- Ask them what they think they have come to school for.
- Find out what they like doing – try to incorporate something of their interest in the activity.
- Show interest in their achievements.
- If they are upset, try to understand why.
- Make sure where they work is comfortable.
- Make sure the tools they are using, including the pencils and paper, are of appropriate quality to do what is needed.
- Ask questions and try not to give answers.
- Help the pupil to do it for themselves.
- Make sure they know the purpose of any task, and ask them what they have learnt at the end of it.
- Praise hard work, attempting activities as well as achieving end results.
- Listen and watch – only interfere if you need to.
- Discuss what goes on with colleagues.
- Watch colleagues at work and pick up ideas that seem to work and try them out.

To help assist learning you can:

- Try to understand more about your own learning styles.
- Provide opportunities for repetition and reinforcement, vocabulary and scaffolding.
- Learn more about the social, cultural or emotional context in which the pupils are operating.

- Find out more about the individual needs of the pupils with whom you are working closely.
- Find out what experiences the learners have already had or what they might have missed.
- Learn something of the subjects that they are learning for yourself, so that you know what might be coming next or know what an appropriate strategy for that subject might be.
- Notice what kind of learning styles pupils have and talk with them about their own learning.
- Value pupils and their learning, appreciate what individuals have achieved and tell them – boost their self-esteem.
- Be authentic and open with pupils and adults.
- Ensure you know what is the learning intention of the teacher.
- Assist in creating a positive learning environment, both in the material surroundings and in attitudes to work and each other.
- Be part of the learning organisation that is your school, share your ideas and listen to others.
- Apply your learning to the situation in which you find yourself.
- Have high expectations of the pupils, yourself and learning standards.

(Watkinson 2002: 44)

Learning objectives

It can be seen from the above that it is important to know the pupils with whom you will be working in order to understand their needs but it is equally important to recognise why the pupil is in school at all – hopefully it is to learn something. This will depend on the curriculum of the school – what is to be learnt and how the teacher interprets the curriculum demands for the particular pupil. This will be set out in writing in the teacher's planning as a 'learning objective' [2-3.1:v; 2-3.2:i]. It may be that this is the same for all the class for all the lesson, and your part in it, or it may be subdivided according to the needs of the pupils or the various parts of the lesson. It makes a great difference as to how you do the task. For instance, an objective of close observational drawing of a flower is different from an imaginative interpretation, a picture exploring colour different from one exploring use of collage materials. It is your role to support the teacher in his or her objectives [2-3.2:1]. Some of the more direct strategies will be discussed in Chapter 7 Supporting the teacher. Your role is to provide support for learning activities as directed by the teacher. This chapter ends with a planning sheet used by teachers (Figure 5.1) setting out the learning objectives for individual children, where differing objectives will be tackled with differing methods.

Child   Week Beginning

Learning Objective	Delivery Method	Outcome
General Comments		

Figure 5.1   A planning sheet for an individual child
© Source: Maldon: Primary School, Essex

6 Providing for similarities and differences of pupils

Inclusion – principles and practice

The move for inclusion in education has developed from a worldwide move towards recognising human rights and counteracting segregation including apartheid and other forms of ethnic cleansing. For some, the word 'inclusion' has come to mean the wholesale closing of special schools, set up to serve the pupils in most need of special education whether their needs are physical or in areas of learning. In practice, pupils with special educational needs are increasingly being included in mainstream education, with arrangements made to ensure their special needs are met. Special schools are still providing education and sources of expertise in various areas, such as those with profound learning, behavioural or physical disabilities, including deafness and visual disabilities, but increasingly these schools are working in tandem with mainstream schools. Mainstream schools sometimes also have special units attached to them with specialist staff in a limited area of disability, where pupils are included in as many mainstream school activities as possible, but withdrawn for certain specialist lessons to the unit. Often pupils are bussed to such units from a wider area than the general catchment area for only one or two years to enable the pupils to get closer specialist attention than possible in, say, a small rural school. The pupils then return to their own area school more able to cope with the general curriculum.

The government Green Paper *Excellence for all Children* (DfEE 1998a) set out the vision 'for increasing the level and quality of inclusion with mainstream schools, while protecting and enhancing specialist provision for those who need it' (p. 43). After consultation *Meeting Special Educational Needs – A programme of action* (DfEE 1998b) was produced followed by a new code of practice for those working in schools (DfES 2001a).

Inclusion does not just happen by a school admitting pupils with particular needs whom it has not admitted in the past, it will mean changes in attitude by some people in the school, always a lengthy process, changes in the learning environment and resource provision [2-1.1:iii]. It may mean the appointment of special assistants to support the learner. Ramps or lifts may be needed for wheelchairs, or visual aids or computers. The SEN and Disability Act 2001 requires every governing body of a maintained school to have an 'accessibility plan' in place by April 2003. If specialist advisers need to visit someone will have to liaise with them, there may be timetabling reorganisation, rewritten job descriptions. Integrating pupils has sometimes meant admitting pupils with needs and then segregating them from their peers for specialist treatment. The very appointment of a special assistant can label a pupil as different which would not have occurred in a special school. Inclusion does not just mean access to curriculum entitlement but including pupils socially and emotionally. Each school should have a policy saying how the school promotes and operates inclusive provision, and will be inspected as to how it performs against this policy [2-2.1:ii]. You must make yourself aware as to how you fit into this scheme of things [2-2.1:ii].

Schools should also have policies saying how they will promote disability awareness, equal opportunities and celebrate multicultural diversity. These may also have implications for your practice in dealing with individual pupils. Withdrawing a pupil from assembly for extra reading, or from PE for regular physiotherapy may or may not be the best use of the time for the pupil, and may have implications as to access to the full curriculum. You must follow the directions of the class teacher or SENCO in such matters. If you find you and particular children are becoming excluded from activities by working away from the rest of the class, have a word with the teacher directing you and find out whether you can work with the group closer to the main class, or could vary the times of your sessions so that your group becomes more part of the general class work. As this might mean a reorganisation of resources or timetable, do this tactfully. If you are concerned, discuss this always with the class teacher or your mentor [2-2.2:i; 2-3.1:ii]. Your role is often to support social relationships between pupils with difficulties or disabilities and their more able peers, enabling them to interact and communicate as the more able peers would with each other. You can enable them to work and play together by your sensitive support, without drawing attention to the problems. A continually hovering adult only makes matters worse, but appropriate intervention, a word in the right place at the right time, could help [2-2.1:iii].

Case study: Good practice

John Bream Secondary School is on two floors and has several separate buildings. It has lifts at various points. Sometimes a TA is delegated just to ensure a wheelchair-bound pupil can get from lesson to lesson quickly enough. Midday support ensures physically disabled pupils can have assistance with feeding in the main dining area, alongside their friends. Physiotherapy done by TAs is timetabled for lunch-hours. Children with learning problems are supported by TAs in class who help pupils with all abilities within the class. To ensure this happens appropriately, discussion meetings between all TAs and selected heads of departments are held weekly to discuss pupils' needs. Timetabling of TAs is constantly reviewed in the light of these joint meetings. Any one student may have assistance from several TAs in a day or week. Individual teachers ensure brief joint planning sessions before lessons and informal feedback after lessons. The SENCO also has regular training sessions with the TAs and the special needs teachers also employed by the school, about appropriate techniques for supporting learning. Some TAs with specialist skills are allocated where they can best be used – a drama graduate TA to the performing arts faculty, an Urdu speaker to the English department to assist with newly arrived students from Pakistan, an ex-professional football player to the PE department. TAs are included in SEN reviews and some liaise directly with parents or specialist advisers such as the physiotherapist. Pupils are rarely withdrawn from classes but may be allocated different homework or tasks within the ordinary lessons. TAs where required oversee the homework diaries with students for whom writing is laborious. Homework facilities are available after school in the ICT suite and library for those with home study problems. Teaching staff and TAs discuss students informally on many occasions, and discuss social and emotional needs with the students, sometimes in formally timetabled group sessions. The school employs trained counsellors part time, and some TAs are trained in modest counselling techniques by them.

Special educational needs

The Code of Practice quotes from Section 312, Education Act 1996:

Children have special educational needs if they have a *learning difficulty* which calls for *special educational provision* to be made for them.
Children have a *learning difficulty* if they:

(a) have a significantly greater difficulty in learning than the majority of children of the same age; or
(b) have a disability which prevents or hinders them from making use of educational facilities of a kind generally provided for children of the same age in schools within the area of the local education authority;
(c) are under compulsory school age and fall within the definition at (a) or (b) above or would so do if special educational provision was not made for them.

Children must not be regarded as having a learning difficulty solely because the language or form of language of their home is different from the language in which they will be taught.

Special educational provision means:

(a) for children of two or over, educational provision which is additional to, or otherwise different from, the educational provision made generally for children of their age in schools maintained by the LEA, other than special schools, in the area;
(b) for children under two, educational provision of any kind.

(DfES 2001: 6)

It goes on to define disability:

A child is disabled if he is blind, deaf or dumb or suffers from a mental disorder of any kind or is substantially and permanently handicapped by illness, injury or congenital deformity or such other disability as may be prescribed.

(Section 17 (11), Children Act 1989)

A person has a disability for the purposes of this Act if he has a physical or mental impairment which has a substantial and long-term adverse effect on his ability to carry out normal day-to-day activities.

(Section 1 (1), Disability Discrimination Act 1995, cited in DfES 2001: 7).

Statementing and Individual Education Plans

In order to ensure the pupils with SEN or disabilities have as equal an opportunity of education as other pupils, special provision is made for them and it is often that TAs are part of that special provision. However, this very fact can be counterproductive and it is up to the teacher and yourself to ensure that the provision is appropriate and does not make the pupils stand out instead of become more part of the school community. If you stick close by your named pupil (sometimes called the 'Velcro' model) this can label your 'charge' as being different, or the pupils can become more dependent on help rather than more independent – one of the aims of providing help.

The Code of Practice (DfES 2001a) clearly sets out the procedures for identification, assessment and provision for pupils with SEN. These need not worry you in great detail but you may well be asked to provide evidence for assessment procedures or carry out some of the specialist provision for identified pupils. Teachers and the SENCO will have decided what action should be taken, but you should always report any concerns you have to the class teacher if nothing has been mentioned to you. There are stages in the response of the school to pupils with SEN. Some schools have an in-house system for identifying pupils of concern at an early stage within the class. The first stage in the Code of Practice is for the school to decide whether a particular *School Action* needs to be taken in addition to or different from the normal provision for pupils at the school. They will have collected all sorts of evidence which will be entered into the school records and have contacted the parents of the pupil. This action may mean some additional one-to-one tuition, often undertaken by a TA. The agreed strategies to be undertaken will be recorded in an Individual Education Plan (IEP) which will also set out targets to achieve, a timetable and process for review and possible success or exit criteria. The three pages of an IEP recommended for use by Essex County Council are shown in Figures 6.1, 6.2 and 6.3.

If the school, in consultation with the parents and if possible the pupil themselves (sometimes the TA is included if they have valuable insight into the pupil's condition or lack of progress), believes that advice or provision from outside the school facilities is required, the stage is called *School Action Plus.* External support services will usually then come to see the pupil and their records. A new IEP will be drawn up, and the delivery of the strategies remains the responsibility of the class teacher (in primary schools) or subject teacher (in secondary schools). The provision should at least in part and wherever possible be undertaken within the normal classroom setting. A pupil who has difficulty

Essex County Council Learning Services		Individual Education Plan & Review
	School: DfES number:	Essex School Action/Essex School Action Plus/ Pastoral Support Programme/ Statement Interim Reviews
Name: Class: **DoB:** Year: **Parent/Carer:** **SENCO/Keyworker:** **Teacher/Form tutor:**		**Previous three review dates:** **Date started:** 1. **ESA** 2. **ESA+** 3. **Statement** **Date of review:** **Next review date:**
Summary of pupil's strengths and achievements:		**Long-term objectives:** (these should be reflected in the short-term objectives/targets)
Summary of pupil's difficulties/needs: (including NC, RA, baseline assessment etc.)		**Pupil management strategies including advice from outside agencies:**
	Evidence attached: ☐	Advice attached: ☐

Cc Parent/s/Carers ☐   Pupil ☐   SENCO ☐   Class Teacher/s ☐   Teaching Assistants ☐   Head of Year ☐   Other ☐   File ☐

Figure 6.1   Page 1 of an Individual Education Plan
© Source: Essex County Council Learning Services

INDIVIDUAL EDUCATION PLAN & REVIEW

Name of pupil: **Date of plan:**   **Date of next plan:**

Objectives/targets planned with parents and pupils

Long-term objectives (across the curriculum)	Current level (From previous IEP progress)	Short-term objectives/targets and success criteria	Strategies (e.g. methods, materials used, frequency, when, who is involved)	Progress (to be completed before next review) Teacher/subject:

Cc Parent/s/Carers ☐   Pupil ☐   SENCO ☐   Class Teacher/s ☐   Teaching Assistants ☐   Head of Year ☐   Other ☐   File ☐

Figure 6.2   Page 2 of an Individual Education Plan
© Source: Essex County Council Learning Services

Record of Provision, Parent and Pupil Views

Name of pupil: Date of review

Present at review: Pupil/student present ☐   Parent/carer invited ☐   Parent/carer present ☐   Review by telephone ☐

Support	From (role)	Time (per week)	Parent/carer view/contribution to plan:
Individual			
Whole class			
Small group (size ....)			Parent's/carer's signature:
Whole School Provision			**Pupil/student view:**
Specific resources (e.g. pencil grip, furniture)	**Internal support/Advice** SENCO Teaching Assistant Other (please specify) **Outside agency advice/support:** Behaviour Support Child/Family Consultation Service Educational Psychologist/Assistant Educational Psychologist Education Welfare Officer Integrated Support Services Social Services Specialist Teacher		Pupil's/student's signature: _____ **SENCO comments**

Future Action: Continue ☐   Cease ☐   Move to Action/Action Plus ☐   Seek advice from outside agency ☐

Cc Parent/s/Carers ☐   Pupil ☐   SENCO ☐   Class Teacher/s ☐   Teaching Assistants ☐   Head of Year ☐   Other ☐   File ☐

Figure 6.3   Page 3 of an Individual Education Plan
© Source: Essex County Council Learning Services

in reading may not only benefit from a DT class, through their own achievement, but may have a greater ability with tools than a pupil who can read fluently – they then experience success and have raised self-esteem. Where possible, particularly where practical work is undertaken, mixed ability groups allow opportunities for sharing and discussion, role modelling and understandings to develop which otherwise are lost. Figure 6.4 is an example of a completed School Action Plus IEP (with the pupil's name removed).

There are a very few pupils where even Action Plus change is not resulting in sufficient progress. It will then be necessary, with the permission of the parents and consultation with those working with the pupils, for a request to be made of the LEA for a statutory assessment to be made. The LEA will consider all the written evidence submitted by the school, and decide whether a statement should be made. This statement will include details of the provision needed by the pupil, and may identify extra resources that will be required. LEAs have funding to allocate for such cases, and statutory (legal) duties to fulfil to ensure these resources are properly used, so monitoring arrangements have to be set up as well. If the LEA decides not to issue a statement, they have to send a written note to the parents telling them why. The final statement includes all the evidence submitted by the school, and the advice given from all the external agencies involved, as well as the educational placement and provision, and any non-educational needs that have to be met. There are processes of consultation, a final statement, methods of appeal and annual review

Individual Education Plan September 2002					

7DS

School Action +

IEP No. 1
Review Date

DOB   07.11.90

Targets to be achieved	Achievement Criteria	Possible resources and techniques	Possible class strategies	Support ideas	Outcome
1 To stop and think before acting.	1 In lessons, registration and about school each week.	1 Discussion. Sequencing cards/stories based on consequences of actions.	1 Discuss acceptable behaviour. Talk about consequences. Praise efforts.	1 Help .... to think about the consequences of actions. Teach temper-controlling techniques.	1
2 To sustain attention until a task is completed	2 Completes task without distraction 1+ times each lesson and registration.	2 Praise. Set achievable tasks. Variety of ways of recording.	2 Present work in a variety of ways. Break tasks down into small steps. Reward ....'s achievement.	2 Discuss tasks. Ensure that .... knows what is required.	2
3 To start a task straight away.	3 Work is begun immediately 1+ times each lesson/registration	3 Achievable tasks set. Reward chart. Self-monitoring form. Achievement stickers.	3 Give clear directions. Encourage .... to complete achievable tasks. Reward success.	3 Ensure that .... understands the task and has any necessary equipment. Praise.	3

Parents/carers need to

Student needs to Think before acting. Focus on tasks. Settle to work quickly.

Copy for parent / teacher / support / file

Figure 6.4   An Action Plus IEP completed
© Source: Stewards School, Harlow, Essex

systems all linked to the process. This creates a considerable amount of paper and use of time for many people and so is not undertaken lightly. A provision named in the statement is also statutory. All pupils in a special school will be there as a result of a statement being made, that such a school was in the pupils' best interest. So if you work in a special school, the processes here will have been completed and annual reviews will take place for all pupils.

The Code of Practice (DfES 2001a) also designates four main areas of need which are likely to be recognised, but these areas quite clearly are not hard and fast.

It recognises, as LEAs will recognise that each child is unique . . . should reflect the particular circumstances of that child . . . that there is a wide spectrum of special educational needs that are frequently inter-related, although there are specific needs that usually relate directly to particular types of impairment.

(p. 85)

Individuals may well be in more than one area. In some cases, a pupil's needs are complex and also severe. The four areas are:

- Communication and interaction
- Cognition (knowing) and learning
- Behaviour, emotional and social development
- Sensory and/or physical

73

If you are working with pupils whom you feel have special needs

When you are settled in post, with the agreement of a class or subject teacher:

- Start with one pupil whose records you have not seen.
- Note as many characteristics as you can that are similar to other pupils' in the class, e.g. can walk, use a pencil, does not need glasses etc.
- Then note the characteristics that make you feel they have special needs.
- Do they have needs in any of the areas above?
- What has the teacher said about them?
- What do you do to help?

Ensure you keep your notes secure, discuss all of them with the teacher and dispose of them with the advice of that teacher.

You may be helping a pupil with specific needs and should know what is required by the IEP or any behaviour plan so that you can have the same aims in your support as the teachers and other assistants [2-2.1:iv; 2-2.2:ii]. You may want to know more about the condition or the needs to know how best to help that pupil. A useful brief description of the most common needs along with your possible actions and some related support associations can be found in the TA File for secondary schools (DfES 2001b: 5.2–5.22). The SENCO will be a good source of information or you can type the condition you are interested in into a search engine on the Internet, or enquire at the local library. Most disabilities have associations, often with local branches to support those disadvantaged or their parents. It is not necessary at an ordinary competent TA level (Level 2) to have an in-depth understanding of various disabilities or needs. What you need is an awareness of what is normal for pupils of the age range you are working with, what is unusual and what might change or cause changes.

There are various ways in which you can support any pupil, whether or not they have SEN. Some pupils just need a bit of individual attention. Some are shy in large groups, some slower to understand what is required and some just take longer to do things. Some need to repeat tasks several times before 'the penny drops'. Sometimes they come from large or busy families where few people, particularly the adults, have time to talk with them, and more particularly to listen to their point of view [2-5.1:3].

You may need to [2-5.1 & 2:2]:

- repeat the teacher's instructions
- simplify or restructure the task indicated by the teacher a little
- read a worksheet
- help the pupil plan out or organise their work
- ensure the pupil concentrates on the task
- suggest where equipment or materials can be found
- suggest another way to do the task

- allow the pupil the opportunity to talk their thinking through
- listen to what the pupil has to say or ask
- get the pupil to check for errors in their work before you point them out
- ask the pupil about the task, what they have found out or learnt
- help the pupil to see what they have done well, enabling them to measure their own success
- ensure they tidy up
- or a combination of some or all of these.

You have got to learn how to balance the pupil's need for attention with the principle of enabling all pupils to become as independent of you as possible – your real job is to do yourself out of a job [2-2.1:3]. The aim is to promote independent learning. This balance is an art which you will acquire if you are sensitive [2-2.1:vi]. Always try to return a question with a question, even 'What do you think?' Encourage pupils to get resources rather than wait on them, to have a go at a task rather than just saying 'I can't do that.' Sometimes the individual attention is due to particular needs, largely physical, that need your help. Personal hygiene needs of a pupil should have been spelt out to you in your induction. You may need to remind a pupil to wear their glasses, or adjust aids for hearing impaired pupils. In these cases you should also have had training as to how to carry out your task [2-2.1:4]. You may provide an escort for a pupil who has to go to see a specialist visitor, possibly even delegated to do so by the parent or carer.

It is more likely that you will be working with pupils in small groups, where individuals in need of special support are one of the group [2-3.2:ii]. In this way, the individual needs are less obvious, you are able to keep an eye on your 'charge' without being oppressive. Group working can be of two kinds. Sometimes pupils just sit in a group for convenience, but actually they all have individual tasks to complete. Here it may be that you just need to keep them on task. However, one of the ways to help them is to get them to finish a little before the intended time, and share their findings or what they have got out of the task. If one has to talk about one's learning, it usually makes that learning 'stick' better. Often members of the group can learn from each other or help each other in a way that promotes the learning of all parties. Sometimes groups are put together and need to work as a group. If they have to discuss something you can act as chairperson, prompting the shy and reticent, making sure everyone has an opportunity to share their ideas, and that all but the speaker listen. Being part of a group may be part of an individual pupil's IEP [2-2.1:2]. You can encourage cooperation and interaction and facilitate discussions. It is a great opportunity to role model how people can work together, also for promoting self-esteem by suitable praise [2-2.2:1]. Never go overboard on praise; pupils know when they have tried hard or a piece of work really could be better.

Your role with the group may be direct teaching – explaining a point, demonstrating a practical task or giving some new information. You should have been briefed by the teacher and been able to prepare. There is more about

Beehive Lane Community Primary School
LSA Working Document

on the IEP for .... Year ....

LSA ....

Targets

Time Span

Activities

Resources

Comments and Evaluation

Figure 6.5   A TA working document for an IEP
© Source: Beehive Lane Community Primary School, Great Baddow, Essex

working with teachers in the next chapter. Figure 6.5 is an example of a planning sheet for a TA.

It is possible that you will be asked to work with a whole class while the teacher carries out a task with an individual. Be careful if this happens. You are not qualified nor paid and possibly not insured to teach a whole class, although you can be an adult in a classroom in an emergency while a teacher is found. If the task is something simple, like reading a story to the class, make sure the teacher is within call or eyesight – they are responsible for the class. You may have a skill as a potter or musician which you can demonstrate to a whole class, again making sure a qualified teacher is around.

If problems arise, you must tell the teacher, your line manager or the SENCO depending on the problem. It may be that pupils have misbehaved with you, or revealed something about other pupils which is important. They may have problems with the tasks set, or just not got on with the task properly. The fault may lie with your techniques with the pupils, or the match of task and pupil, or the emotional state of the pupil. It needs to be sorted quickly so that it does not become habitual [2-2.1:xi].

At the end of a lesson, a week or a term, you may be asked to complete aspects of pupil records, or write a contribution for these records [2-1.2]. Always do this under directions. Be concise and accurate. Always ensure that the records or notes are kept confidentially, stored appropriately in a secure place. It is most likely that you will only do this on the school premises anyway.

Communication and interaction [2-2.1:v]

The Code of Practice defines this area of difficulty as follows:

7:55 Most children with special educational needs have strengths and difficulties in one, some or all of the areas of speech, language and communication. Their communication needs may be both diverse and complex. They will need to continue to develop their linguistic competence in order to support their thinking as well as their communication. The range of difficulties will encompass children and young people with speech and language delay, impairments or disorders, specific learning difficulties, such as dyslexia and dyspraxia, hearing impairment and those who demonstrate features within the autistic spectrum; they may also apply to some children and young people with moderate, severe or profound learning difficulties. The range of need will include those for whom language and communication difficulties are the result of permanent sensory or physical impairment.

7.56 These children may require some, or all, of the following:
• flexible teaching arrangements
• help in acquiring, comprehending and using language
• help in articulation
• help in acquiring literacy skills
• help in using augmentative and alternative means of communication
• help to use different means of communication confidently and competently for a range of purposes, including formal situations
• help in organising and coordinating oral and written language
• support to compensate for the impact of a communication difficulty on learning in English as an additional language
• help in expressing, comprehending and using their own language, where English is not the first language.

(DfES 2001a: 86)

One special need of which you need to be aware is that of language, if the pupil comes from a home where English is not the language of communication. They may need help in interpreting the nuance of some words, especially where the teacher has given instructions in technical language or speaks quickly. Another sensitivity you must show is towards those who have different cultures from yourself. This is not necessarily associated with race or colour, it could be due to religion or region or even class. Always discuss any concerns you have with your mentor, line manager or the teacher. There is more about supporting aspects of English or literacy in Chapter 8.

> **To communicate effectively you need to:**
>
> - Try to understand the needs of the person with whom you are speaking.
> - Show and expect respect.
> - Listen well.
> - Speak or write clearly, with correct English grammar (you may need to slow down, but shouting does not help).
> - Use vocabulary appropriate to the age and learning stage of the listener.
> - Keep to the point.
> - Share ideas.
> - Smile and use humour and praise appropriately.
> - Be relaxed, warm, friendly and supportive.
> - Keep eye contact.
> - Be positive.

Cognition and learning

The Code of Practice defines this area of difficulty as follows:

> **7:58** Children who demonstrate features of moderate, severe or profound learning difficulties or specific learning difficulties, such as dyslexia or dyspraxia, require specific programmes to aid progress in cognition and learning. Such requirements may also apply to some extent to children with physical and sensory impairments and those on the autistic spectrum. Some of these children may have associated sensory, physical and behavioural difficulties that compound their needs. These children may require some, or all, of the following:
>
> - flexible teaching arrangements
> - help with processing language, memory and reasoning skills
> - help and support in acquiring literacy skills
> - help in organising and coordinating spoken and written English to aid cognition
> - help with sequencing and organisational skills
> - help with problem solving and developing concepts
> - programmes to aid improvement of fine and motor competencies
> - support in the use of technical terms and abstract ideas
> - help in understanding ideas, concepts and experiences when information cannot be gained through first hand sensory or physical experiences.
>
> (DfES 2001a: 86–87)

You can see that many of the requirements of the pupils with needs in this area are similar to those with communication or interactive difficulties, but the emphasis is on organisational and coordinating skills, concept development and problem solving. Many of these skills though are mediated through language, including specific language to handle more abstract ideas. Your role modelling of utilising correct nomenclature for things, and organisation will help pupils, particularly in the more technical subjects like science. Emphasise working sequentially, one thing at a time, and tidying up properly. Allow older pupils to use concrete materials – counters for number work for instance, or draw pictures of objects if you do not have them to hand, if they are having problems with working in the abstract. Most of the strategies that are used to support the learning of pupils younger than the one with which you are concerned will be useful, so you can ask teachers of the younger pupils how they would tackle certain areas of the curriculum if it is appropriate to do so. You should ask the teacher with whom you are working if this is all right, as a matter of courtesy.

Many of the concepts like hot and cold, hard and soft are usually learnt through play activities in the early years. These are developed in science lessons in the properties of materials, as are the more difficult concepts like forces, electricity, growth and change.

Some specific programmes have been developed to help disorganised pupils to organise themselves, but use of these is likely to be part of an IEP. You should receive training if asked to implement such programmes.

Behaviour, emotional and social development

The Code of Practice defines this area of difficulty as follows:

> **7:60** Children and young people who demonstrate features of emotional and behavioural difficulties, who are withdrawn or isolated, disruptive and disturbing, hyperactive and lack concentration; those with immature social skills; and those presenting challenging behaviours arising from other complex special needs, may require help or counselling for some, or all, of the following:
>
> - flexible teaching arrangements
> - help with development of social competence and emotional maturity
> - help in adjusting to school expectations and routines
> - help in acquiring the skills of positive interaction with peers and adults
> - specialised behavioural and cognitive approaches
> - re-channeling or re-focusing to diminish repetitive and self-injurious behaviours
> - provision of class and school systems which control or censure negative or difficult behaviours and encourage positive behaviour
> - provision of a safe and supportive environment.
>
> (DfES 2001a: 87)

Behaviour management

It is possible that you have been appointed to assist in the support of a pupil who has problems with conforming to the expected behaviour patterns of the school, thus disrupting the work of other pupils and not learning well themselves. But, for whatever reason you have been appointed, you must become part of the whole school's system for behaviour management. It is no good only certain adults maintaining discipline, pupils needs to understand that all adults will reinforce the codes by which the school maintains order. While this book can merely touch on the essentials, you will find Fox's (2001) book much more detailed and helpful. Wherever possible try to get some local training in this area. Senior members of staff will always be available for you if a situation becomes more than you should deal with, either to refer matters to at the time or later for advice. Schools also have access to specialist teams and psychologists to whom you may be able to talk. There will be courses available both within the school INSET programme and externally delivered. Discuss with your mentor what would be most suitable for your needs [3-1.2:ix].

All schools have policies and procedures that all staff must follow, the importance factor being consistency of approach whatever the incident [2-2.2:v; 3-1.1:i]. Some of the policies that do not directly give guidance about behaviour management are also important in this area [3-1.1:ii; 3-1.2:i]. For instance, if you withdraw a pupil from class because he or she is behaving badly, you are depriving him or her of that part of the curriculum but sometimes it has to be done; restraining a pupil could be construed as child abuse; dealing with bullying may be in a separate policy. You must know the limits of your authority, when and to whom you refer incidents outside that authority, your particular role within the school and the roles of others [2-2.2:5; 3-1.1:iii & 2:iii]. As you become more experienced you may see situations or learn of strategies that could be introduced to your school but are not currently available. Again, talk with your mentor or line manager about them, and feed them back in any in-house training sessions for discussion [3-1.2:7].

Rogers (1991) has some useful things to say about discipline and behaviour:

Decisive discipline is marked by these characteristics:

- a focus on the due rights of all
- an assertive stance

(Assertion is distinguished between aggression and hostility on the one hand, and passivity or capitulating to student demands on the other. Essentially, assertion communicates one's own need and due rights without trampling on the other parties' rights.)

- refusal to rely on power or role-status to gain respect
- speaking and acting respectfully even when frustrated or angry
- choosing to respond to discipline incidents (from prior reflection and planning) rather than reacting to incidents as they arise
- preparing for discipline as rigorously as any aspect of the curriculum.

When actually disciplining, a decisive approach engages the student by:

- establishing eye contact
- speaking clearly with appropriate firmness
- speaking briefly, addressing primary behaviour and ignoring as much of the secondary behaviour as is possible
- distinguishing between the child and his or her behaviour
- expecting compliance rather than demanding or merely hoping for it
- re-establishing working relationships as soon as possible.

(p. 43)

You must quickly learn what is acceptable behaviour in the various areas of the school and what is not, how to identify pupils in difficulties and what is normal [3-1.1:4]. Negative behaviour may be verbal or physically abusive or offensive. Racial or sexist actions or language should not be tolerated. Bullying needs to be recognised and dealt with. Try to spot signs of potential conflict – it is more easily dealt with in the early stages, then monitor developments. You must also recognise that sometimes circumstances change, both for pupils and the school, and be alert to these changes [3-1.1:vi]. Changing rooms or buildings or going from inside the school to the playground or sports field can alter behaviour. In order to learn all this you will need to understand the limits of normal behaviour and have copies of the policies and procedures for your school on dealing with what, for the school, is inappropriate behaviour. Go through them with a mentor or line manager to identify your role and appropriate strategies [2-3.2:iii; 3-1.2:1].

Behaviour patterns develop as do other aspects of physical and mental development. Emotional and social development also take place so expectations of behaviour will vary with the age of the pupils. Physical changes such as those experienced by pupils going through puberty can alter their behaviour radically, as any parent of this age child will know. Peer pressure can make an otherwise well-behaved child do something out of character, such as play truant or cheek a teacher [3-1.1:7]. In some cultures, some behaviour is acceptable for boys but not girls. This can sometimes be seen in early years settings where rough play is acceptable for boys, but girls will be admonished for similar behaviour. We can all have assumptions of what is appropriate, depending on our own upbringing. For instance, many people still have the idea that young people with severe learning problems do not have sexual urges; they do, and can fall in love just like more able youngsters. The paraplegic athletes have challenged our ideas of physical capacity in recent years [3-1.1:viii]. What is age appropriate in an infant school pupil may be considered inappropriate in a secondary school pupil yet some secondary pupils may behave in an infantile way, expressing their feelings or emotions in coping with a problem. While you will aim to respond to the older pupil hoping they will respond in a more mature way, in responding to their behaviour rather than them personally you may need to modify your actions. You need to accommodate the pupil according to his or her level of development and this will probably need you to discuss your actions with your mentor or line manager and find out more about the pupil.

It is also important to recognise that behaviour management takes place all the time, not just when things go wrong. Thanking, smiling, praising appropriately, all contribute to positive attitudes in relationships [2-2.2:iii; 2-5.1 & 2:3; 3-1.1:1 & v; 3-1.2:vii]. Encouragement is very important for all children, and for adults too. Think back to that personal learning experience suggested in the last chapter, and your own relationships. How much easier it is to work with people who recognise your effort, even if the actual achievement is small. Many of those with learning problems have poor self-esteem and this can be a real drawback when learning, although low self-esteem can affect any ability pupil [3-1.1:vii]. Let them know when they are doing well and show them how close they are to getting the desired outcome. Ask the teacher whether you can write on pupils' work and what kind of comment is acceptable. Specific remarks are much more useful: 'completed quickly' and 'clearer handwriting' say more than 'well done'. Be careful not to do too much for them (no matter how much they wheedle). One of the real problems is that children with poor learning skills can develop a kind of learnt helplessness.

Being pleasant whenever possible means that when you have to correct inappropriate behaviour it has more effect. Role model how you wish children to behave, modulate your voice, walk, do not run, be punctual and polite [3-1.1:2 & iv]. Keep calm (whatever you are feeling inside), listen and be consistent [3-1.1:6; 3-1.2:2]. Respect breeds respect. We all need boundaries so rules are developed [3-1.2:vi]. We all have rights, but we also have responsibilities. This includes access to school facilities, equipment and materials for staff and pupils, and developing responsibility in pupils. The aim is to make pupils take responsibility for their own behaviour [3-1.1:3]. The behaviour management training (DfEE 2000c) talks of the 4Rs approach: Rules, Routines, Rights and Responsibilities leading to choices which have consequences.

Your school may have a systematic reward system, with stickers and certificates for achievements. If so, you will need to know whether you can operate this and what for, and if not how you can best bring achievements to the attention of someone who can do the rewarding. Similarly, there may be sanctions which you can use, such as stopping a pupil misbehaving in the playground and giving them 'time out', or ensuring a particular item gets mentioned in a home dialogue or report book [3-1.1:x]. Usually you are there on the spot to see to the immediate situation, but a more senior member of staff will carry out a punishment such as detention or informing parents [3-1.1:8]. If the situation occurs in the classroom in a lesson, you need to know what to refer to the teacher and what you can deal with [3-1.2:x & 4]. Once you know the ways of the school, you are in a strong position to say to a pupil who might argue with you, 'You have a choice – you can do what you know is right or . . .' whatever the consequence is for that misbehaviour in your school.

Using the language of choice

- It gives children confidence by giving them responsibility
- It regards mistakes as a normal part of learning
- It removes the struggle for power
- It has a positive emphasis
- It is an overt link between principles and strategy.

(DfEE 2000b: 17)

Deal with matters immediately you see inappropriate behaviour [3-1.1:5]. The secret is to be assertive without being aggressive or confrontational and to ensure that you are separating any inappropriate behaviour from the pupil. This enables the pupil to save face and maintain their self-esteem, which is probably low. Keep the focus on the primary behaviour, the thing that drew your attention in the first place, and actively try to build up your relationship with the pupil concerned. Always follow up on things that count: if you have said you will refer the matter to someone else or you will talk to them again on the next day, then be sure you do it. Always seek help if you need it. Try not to get yourself into a situation where you are alone with very challenging pupils. If you see a potential problem situation, make someone else aware and attempt to defuse it [3-1.2:3]. Such a situation can occur with an individual if there is shortage of equipment or a challenging piece of work; or with a group, for instance, in a slow lunch queue. Typical positive strategies include appropriate praise and encouragement [2-2.2:3]. Pupils who are motivated and interested are less likely to misbehave. Do not touch or restrain a pupil in a conflict situation unless you have been specially taught the procedure for your school [2-2.2:5, 6, vi & vii; 3-1.2:ii].

Counselling is a skill. Before you embark on any in-depth work of this kind with pupils, do take advice and if possible training to ensure you know what you are doing.

You need to find out

what is appropriate for:
• classrooms. Different teachers' classrooms will vary slightly
• within other areas of the school
• outside the school premises
• laboratories or technical areas
• individuals
• groups
• whole classes

what are:
• the rules [3-1.2:vi]
• the rewards and sanctions that can be applied
  – by you
  – by others [3-1.2:v]

what strategies are available for you to use in managing inappropriate behaviour [3-1.2:viii]:
• time out places
• sources of help and referral at different times of the day
• report forms or notes
• withdrawal of privileges

how you:
• report incidents
• develop your skills of behaviour management
• seek advice

Individual pupils may have individual targets, plans and performance indicators similar to those of a pupil with learning difficulties, called Behaviour Support Plans [3-1.2:iv]. If you are likely to come into contact with such a pupil, you must acquaint yourself with these. The targets will be small, such as to keep the pupil on task for ten minutes. Your aim will not be to take responsibility for, cure or independently change the pupil's behaviour. There will be the equivalent of an IEP for behaviour, showing what you are to do, and usually any paperwork of which you have copies will have a space for you to comment on progress [3-1.2:5 & 6]. As the pupil will know their targets, any comments about progress that you might make to the pupil can also relate to the target, such as 'You didn't interrupt the lesson today, well done, let's see if you can do it again tomorrow.'

Case study: Good behaviour management

An infant school in a very poor social area, where few children received preschool education apart from the school nursery class, had also had low expectations of behaviour and academic standards in the past. Over some years, the new head established a positive behaviour management regime which enabled the whole school to become a happy and learning establishment. It took time to establish the ethos and train all sectors of the staff to understand the detailed approach. Each teacher had their own TA. The two became a small team, and the teaching staff had away days sometimes incorporating team-building exercises. Over several years teaching staff went to summer schools in their own time to undertake specific training in positive techniques which were incorporated in their classroom practice with their TAs. This even included practice sessions, with agreed prompt phrases pinned inside cupboard doors. Later, as classroom support staff became converted to the particular way of dealing with all the children, office, caretaking and midday staff were trained. Money was put into resource organisation such as shelves, labelled boxes, sufficient and quality tools, materials and equipment to enable children to organise themselves and take responsibility for their own learning. Playground equipment and activities were organised; joint curriculum planning reflected the whole-school ethos. Even the youngest had to plan some of their own work, and all children helped in cleaning up. Children were thanked for walking, assemblies were quiet, disciplined affairs. Parents become aware of the calm and even started to emulate the staff's attitudes and phrases while on the school site. Test results began to climb as the philosophy of high expectations permeated the formal curriculum.

Bullying

This is a particular concern of many pupils and parents. No school is without its bullies and the nature of bullying is that it will take place away from adult sight, so may be hard to detect. 'Bullying is forcing others to do, act and feel the very things a bully would never want done to him. Bullying is not accidental, it is learned.' Schools have policies for dealing with bullying issues, as there need to be 'clear, school-wide consequences' (Rogers 1994: 101). There should not only be strategies for dealing with the bully, but also for helping the victim, both in the short term and in the long term, to become more assertive. It is likely that pupils will debate the issue in class and strategies like circle time be available to help. These are probably run by the teachers, but you may be asked to undertake training in this area to run such sessions as well as participate in discussions.

Sensory and/or physical needs

The Code of Practice defines this area of difficulty as follows:

> **7:62** There is a wide spectrum of sensory, multi-sensory and physical difficulties. The sensory range extends from profound and permanent deafness or visual impairment through to lesser levels of loss, which may only be temporary. Physical impairments may arise from physical, neurological or metabolic causes that only require appropriate access to educational facilities and equipment; others may lead to more complex learning and social needs; a few children will have multi-sensory difficulties some with associated physical difficulties. For some children the inability to take part fully in school life causes significant emotional stress or physical fatigue. Many of these children and young people will require some of the following:
>
> - flexible teaching arrangements
> - appropriate seating, acoustic conditioning and lighting
> - adaptations to the physical environment of the school
> - adaptations to school policies and procedures
> - access to alternative or augmented forms of communication
> - provision of tactile and kinaesthetic materials
> - access to different amplification systems
> - access to low vision aids
> - access in all areas of the curriculum through specialist aids, equipment or furniture
> - regular and frequent access to specialist support.
>
> (DfES 2001a: 88)

Most of these provisions are specific to the physical impairment of the pupil and you will need specialist training in their use, even if this is fairly informal. All of your support needs to be done with a view to maintaining the pupil's maximum independence within the limits of the disability. Depending on the age of the pupil and the nature of the disability your role might range from one-to-one assistance with a learning task to being on hand to give occasional assistance for learning or personal needs. You will find it very helpful to get information from specialist support associations about the impairment you are supporting. The other thing is that you may be in the best position to spot the early signs of an impairment, such as the need for glasses or deafness. Do tell the appropriate teacher of your concerns, who can then discuss the matter with the parent. You also can help pupils by reminding them to use their aids. Be prepared to meet and discuss the support with any visiting agency as you are in the best position to have seen any aids or materials in use.

7 Supporting the teacher and teaching

The classroom environment

The optimum learning environment is not just safe and healthy. Remember your own learning experiences. You needed the equipment and resources to learn – books, a computer, needles and thread, clay, a car or whatever if it was a conventional course. To study or think or reflect you also need time and opportunity to concentrate. You can study longer if the furniture is correct for posture, the temperature is right and you have had sufficient food, not a large meal. Research is showing that you can think better if you drink water at appropriate intervals and have exercise frequently. Some people learn better with music in the background, some only in the company of others and some need absolute silence. Fear or insecurity does not help. The teacher will set the scene of his or her classroom, creating resource centres, setting out the furniture appropriately and putting up displays to create the atmosphere they feel is most conducive to the tasks to be performed there. Remember, you will always be working under the direction of the teacher who takes responsibility for the learning of the pupils and so also the learning environment [2-1.1:1]. He or she may delegate things to you, that is you may be given a particular role in maintaining the environment, such as display or plants and animals, and they may have other people doing other things, say art media and books, or have specialist technicians for science equipment or ICT, so you need to know how you fit into their scheme of things [2-1.1:i & ii].

Display

Display has several purposes and may include:

- health and safety notices, like the fire escape route, washing hands after handling certain things, or use of potentially dangerous tools;
- ideas for using equipment, like books or computers;
- ideas for work to do if set tasks are finished;
- posters giving general information or pictures of relevant interest to topics being studied;
- pupils' work showing quality presentation, good ideas or just valuing the achievement of class members;

- three-dimensional displays of books or artefacts or models associated with the work of the pupils.

Whatever is displayed and the manner in which it is displayed give messages to people entering the room – pupils and adults – about the purpose of the room, the nature of the work that goes on there, what is valued by the teacher and the school. If displays become faded and tatty, the message is 'who cares?'

It may well be part of your role to renew or create displays for the teacher. You need to know what the intention of the display is, but you also need to learn some skills to help you. For instance, choice of backing paper and ways of framing pupils' two-dimensional work can make a difference to whether the display is eye-catching or not. The kind of lettering and its size matters as well as what is written about the work. Three-dimensional displays can be interactive – allowing pupils to touch and examine objects or just for visual effect. Care with paper trimmers, scissors and glue shows care of pupils' work. Teachers should give you plenty of advice on what they are hoping to achieve; most of them have become very skilled at it. Where possible involve the pupils in ideas of what or how to display their work.

Look at at least three different areas in the school including areas within and outside classrooms

- What display is there? What is it for?
- What condition is it in? How long has it been there?
- Is it looked at by the pupils?
- Is it two or three-dimensional? Why?
- If you feel it is effective, try to note why.
- What colours have been used in addition to the items being displayed?
- What other materials – fabrics, paper, framing have been used?
- Is the display cluttered or relatively bare?
- Are the items in straight lines?
- Is there any explanatory text added by the displayer?
- What tools, equipment or materials might be needed to create such a display – staple gun, pins, scissors, paper trimmer, framing equipment, paper, fabrics, artefacts, books?
- Do you know where to find all of these and how to use them?

If you want to further this interest, look at displays in shop windows, art galleries, museums, advertisements and libraries to pick up ideas on how the displays are made eye-catching or informative. See if there are courses or evening classes in your local centres. Practise with your pictures or ornaments at home.

Making and maintaining equipment, resources and materials

It may also be part of your role to ensure that things are ready for the pupils. Tasks can range from photocopying, making games or worksheets, through to fully fledged technician status in a laboratory, technology department or ICT suite. In these latter cases, you will need specialist training, as the equipment will be specialist, expensive and possibly dangerous. Some further help is given in the next chapter under supporting practical work. You may be given the role of ensuring there are always adequate supplies of basic classroom resources such as paper and pencils and that they are in good condition. Establish a routine of checking, and find out where and how you get renewals [2-1.2:v].

Photocopying

- Ensure you know how to work the machine.
- Check the copyright rules.
- Check the paper tray – and always try to leave it ready for someone else to use who might be in a hurry.
- Can the items be double sided, thus saving paper?
- What will you do if the machine runs out of ink? Stalls? Runs out of paper? Has a paper jam?
- Check the position of the master, the enlargement and select the number of copies needed.
- Do one to start with to check the contrast, then do the run.
- What do you do if the quality is not as you would wish – blurred, pale, streaky?

Creating a tape or disk library

This may be audio or videotape, floppy disk, CD or DVD

- Ensure you know:
    - Where the recorded tapes or disks are to be stored.
    - Where to find blanks [3-17.1:4 & iii; 3-17.2:7& xii].
    - What is to be recorded and that copyright is not infringed.
    - Where the recording equipment is kept and how it is used [3-17.1:2].
    - Whether anyone else wants to use it when you do.
- Practise using the equipment so that you are familiar with it and can record at the correct speed, with the minimum of waste tape or disk space [3-17.2:i].
- Keep full and accurate records of what is recorded, preferably in some kind of publicly available filing system so that teachers can access it easily.
- Label the tapes and disks clearly, possibly also using some kind of numerical or alphabetical code so that they can be returned to their correct places.
- Check the required shelf life of the recording with the teacher requesting the item and reuse tapes and disks whenever possible.

Tools and materials

If you are made responsible for any of these, it could be the paper stock cupboard or scissors, pencils and paint pots or more sophisticated items.

The crucial things are to keep them:

- tidy – check regularly

- accessible to other staff in a hurry – organise them suitably, keep items on shelves or in labelled boxes
- complete and functional – do not let stocks run out, so find out the system for renewal, find out about disposal of broken or torn items
- sharp and safe – find out about maintenance procedures and read all safety precautions
- secure – ensure that expensive items are dealt with as the school wishes, which may be under lock and key or even alarmed

Where possible involve pupils in looking after things and using them properly.

Planning and preparation

Unfortunately, the introduction of TAs to many schools was done as a result of earmarked funding for individual pupils, and the funding came in multiples of pupil contact hours associated with particular pupils. This has led to the 'Velcro' approach to learning support, a misunderstanding about entitlement to provision and TAs paid only for these hours. Effective support cannot take place without some planning, preparation and reflection on the process both by the teacher and the TA [2-3.1:vi]. This needs time outside the pupil contact time although not necessarily a lot. Alternative ways of communication other than meeting can be devised, although dialogue to form proper relationships is also essential. Some schools and LEAs have recognised the need for paid non-contact time for both partners, but still some parents and pupils think that they have to have so many hours one-to-one support each week. The Code of Practice clearly states that 'this may not be the most appropriate way of helping the child' (DfES 2001a: 53). After all, should the most challenging pupils have support from the least experienced and trained member of staff?

Teachers plan for the long term so that pupils do not cover the same material year after year. Together they have developed yearly schemes of work to plan out curriculum coverage over the time the pupils are in the school. It is unlikely that you will need to see or understand these, but you will soon recognise the differences between what goes on in each year group as you work in different classes. The changes are also based on the understanding that pupils learn some things better at different ages. The basic elements of learning to read, write, count and explore systematically will be taught in the earlier years. The junior years, Years 3 to 6, introduce more factual materials and work that needs certain independent fluency with texts and numbers; topic or project work encompasses experimental and explorative work in science and the humanities (history and geography). Skills are taught in the arts and physical education. In secondary schools, Years 7 to 11, subjects are taught separately by specialists often in specialist areas. By Years 12 and 13 (the old sixth forms), pupils are expected to be independent learners able to research texts, question and use skills to an advanced level, whether taking the A level examinations or more vocational courses. The older the pupils are the more they are able to cope with abstract concepts.

Individual teachers or sometimes year groups of teachers then plan for the medium term, usually a term ahead. These plans are usually available and you will find them helpful and interesting. By looking at them you will know what kinds of things will be coming up in the term and whether there are any contributions or ideas you could contribute. There may be field trips or specific activities planned which you could put into your diary. As you get to know the teachers and work with them, they may ask you to join them in composing medium-term plans.

They then produce short-term plans covering the detail of each week's work, how they are adapting the curriculum to the needs of the pupils and how the pupils have been dealing with the work up to date. These plans should incorporate your role in supporting the pupils' learning. Within these short-term plans, they will produce some individual lesson plans. These should contain the learning objectives [2-3.1:v] and some indication of the teacher's expectations of what the outcomes may be [2-5.1:1 & 2:1]. Some examples of planning can be seen in the Literacy and Numeracy Strategy materials; ask your literacy coordinator to show you the materials. Figure 7.1 indicates the planning process in diagrammatic form.

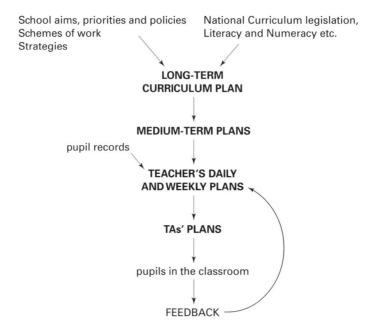

Figure 7.1 Planning strategies

Where managers and teachers are concerned about best practice you will be timetabled and have systems of communication which enable you to understand not only what you have to do before you are to do it, but also why. Schools have a variety of approaches in this area to help you to understand what you are doing. In some instances you may be invited to attend planning meetings. This is a very useful thing to do as it will give you a clear opportunity of hearing what it is the teachers want the children to learn, in particular any specific group you may be working with. Some schools have a TA's folder. This usually lives on the teacher's desk. Teachers use it by writing out for you clear expectations of the work you will be doing in any given session. These instructions may include the names of any children you will be working with in the shared part of the hour and will let you know the kind of support needed. Not every part would be filled in every time as often work is ongoing. Some schools ensure TAs have access to copies of such plans by putting them in folders in the staffroom, in others teachers complete notes in an exercise book or produce a separate TA plan for the lesson. This latter can also include a space in which you can write down what you actually did, and what happened to the pupils while you did it. Did you achieve the teacher's objective with those pupils? This feedback is vital for the teacher to continue planning for the needs of all the pupils in the class and your future role. Examples of planning sheets used in the literacy hour can be found in Chapter 9, but these could be adapted for any lesson.

You need these plans at least the night before, and then you need time (preferably paid) to prepare what you need for the lesson(s) [2-1.1:1 & ii]. The standards ask that you 'offer constructive and timely suggestions as to the support you can provide to a planned activity' (LGNTO 2001, Level 2, p. 13).To do this you will have to have time and opportunity to discuss the teacher's plans with him or her. This can cause a little friction especially in secondary schools if teachers are not used to discussing their planning with anyone. If this does happen, talk it over with your mentor and try to find some strategies to make the suggestions. Stick a polite Post-it note on the teacher's desk when you leave the room, or in the pupil's workbook if the teacher is going to see it – not if it is going home. Make time voluntarily to chat and gradually your contribution will be recognised, meetings will be convened and paid planning time will be instituted. This happens in many schools already.

You may have to find resources, do some photocopying, check out some equipment and its availability, read up about the subject, find some artefacts or reference books for the pupils, or even ask someone what on earth the teacher is getting at [2-3.2:2]. You must ask if you do not understand. If you do not understand, then neither will the pupils [2-3.1:2]. Recognise your limitations, but also use your experience and expertise [2-3.1:iv].

Your standards of planning and preparation will set a standard for the pupils with whom you work [2-3.1:3]. Tatty paper, blunt tools, uninformed you all mean to the pupils that what they do with you does not matter. It needs to matter or you are all wasting your time.

Case study: Good practice in planning and preparation

A TA was working with a Year 4 class. The teacher's plans up in the file in the staffroom indicated that the TA was to work with five less able children in a wet area attached to an open plan classroom. One of the children had recently returned from a speech and language unit having communication problems. The task was to carry out some capacity experiments with various vessels, guessing and measuring. The pupils needed to have more hands-on experience of how shape can alter capacity. It was a mathematics lesson, not a science lesson. The TA realised, from working in the school a few terms, that primary schools now work in litres, not pints as she had done at school. So, after a brief chat with the teacher that evening after school, to check what apparatus was available for her to use, she went home, got out her own measuring jugs and a few containers, and had a go looking at the 'ml' section on the jug, not the 'fluid ounces'. Luckily, her young son came home in the middle of this and she had to explain to him what she was doing – a process which subsequently helped her explain to the pupils in her group what they were to do. She actually wrote down a few words that she found useful in the process. Next morning she felt ready to help the children, got out the equipment while the teacher explained the various tasks to the class and performed the required task with her group. Afterwards, she had a brief word with the class teacher as to which children she felt had grasped the object of the exercise, and the teacher noted this in her planning book.

Pupil contact time

Whatever the planning and preparation, how you actually perform with the pupils in or out of the classroom is going to be the crunch time. This is when your every move and word count [2-3.2:1]. Sometimes this is hard, if you are feeling off colour, or the dog was sick just before you left, or your father rang on the way to school and intends calling in that evening for a meal or the washing machine gave up, but you are now a professional, paid to do a job. At the school gate you have to leave your trouble behind (mentally) and concentrate on being a TA. This may mean acting a part, but all professionals have to do this. If things are really bad, you have had a family bereavement or major upset, then be sure you tell your line manager, who will surely help. You should be appropriately dressed for whatever activities you are planning to do, with aprons, gloves or plimsolls if needed, setting a good example to your pupils, who often try to duck such things. Remember simple things like manners, for instance do not talk with a group of pupils if the teacher is speaking. Always add 'please's and 'thank you's. Work systematically through tasks and ensure you clear up with the pupils, getting them to do all they can.

Many lessons have three parts to them, some more obvious than others – an introduction, possibly with a whole class starter activity, a main activity where pupils get on with some task, and a concluding or plenary section. You may find the following instructions given to TAs in a secondary school helpful.

Teaching assistants and the three-part lesson

Ideally, TAs should be involved in joint planning. If this is not possible, the teacher should make them aware of their plans. In doing so they should outline key questions, key vocabulary and make their expectations clear.

Oral/mental starter

During this part of the lesson, the TA can aid the teacher in the following ways:

- Encouraging reluctant learners to join in
- Focusing on a group of students, giving whispers and prompts

---

- Modeling behaviour – look at teacher, refer to vocabulary on wall
- Alerting teacher if special group have an answer
- Being discrete – some pupils will have low self-esteem

It is also helpful if the TA has the same resources that the teacher is using, perhaps smaller versions.

Main activity

During this part of the lesson, the TA can aid the teacher in the following ways:

- Ensuring that instructions are understood
- Providing really focused teaching with a small group of pupils
- Preparing pupils for the plenary, perhaps helping to report back
- Enabling independence

Plenary

During this part of the lesson, the TA can aid the teacher in the following ways:

- Whispering prompts
- Sitting near less confident pupils
- Encouraging participation
- Mentioning particularly good work   (Source: Stewards School, Harlow)

When you are with the pupils in the main activity, you will actually be teaching in the wider sense of that term. You will be able to give much more individual attention to certain pupils than the teacher, but do ensure the level and type of attention is what the teacher intends and the curriculum requires [2-1.1:1]. For instance, when working with a pupil or two using a computer, it is very tempting to engage in the programme yourself and participate, but it may be that the pupil needs mouse practice rather than just to get the answers to the problems posed. You will enable the pupils to read instructions, explain, instruct, listen, ensure they take turns or share, ensure the quietest get a time to speak and the extrovert gives way to the others at times [2-3.2:1 & 3]. Explain to enable the pupils to do the task more successfully themselves. You can keep them on task without being aggressive, praise their progress, comment on success, assist only where necessary – show by example rather than doing it for them [2-3.2:5 & 8]. You can make things interesting and relevant to their world. Use words they will understand [2-3.1:7]. Get them to read instructions and labels, trying out the spelling of words and drawing their own pictures. Ask open-ended questions like 'Why did you do that?', 'Can you explain what you did?', 'What might happen if you did that again?', 'What do you think about it?' Challenge their ideas where you can to make them think, but always ensure they are not undermined by such questioning. So praise whenever you can, but appropriately.

Always give some kind of feedback to the pupils, maybe something to aim to do better next time. Where possible tell the teacher what you have suggested; again a Post-it note on the planning sheet or the desk or in the pupil's book will do. You should have established whether you are to write directly in pupils' books and the approved method of doing this: red or black pen, comments or ticks, corrections procedures, etc. [2-3.2:iii]. You can say 'You tried hard' or 'That is well done for you', particularly if it fulfilled the teacher's targets for those pupils for that lesson [2-3.1:vii]. Saying 'That is marvellous' when it clearly is not does no one any favours. If the work is careless, particularly if you know them well and they can do better, get them to do it again, or if there is not time, at least recognise that they can do better. Maybe they are having an 'off' day. Try to ensure they finish the task set, giving them a warning as time gets short. If they finish early, they should have some kind of follow-up task to do [2-3.2:7]. You may need to help them complete a homework diary. Always seek help from the teacher if you are unsure what to do [2-3.2:8].

Case study: Good practice in the classroom

James, a TA, had picked up the teacher's planning the day before for the science lesson, and had checked with the technician that he did not have to prepare anything special for the double period the next day. Overnight he had checked details with a school textbook of which he had a copy, and felt prepared for the lesson. As he enters the laboratory he makes eye contact with the teacher, both smile and nod. He slips in beside Alexis, who has recently come to the school and who, while he has a good command of spoken English, is not sure of the written word and still has a limited vocabulary for specialist subjects like science. Alexis does not have severe learning problems, but needs help to achieve the standards expected of his age group. Without this help, he is likely to lose interest and become a behaviour management problem. James makes notes during the teacher's introduction of the practical session. Once the group work starts James goes through his notes with Alexis and checks he knows what to do in the worksheet. James then moves away and is quickly called to another group to assist in their interpretation of the teacher's instructions. About halfway through the session, James is asked by another pupil a question about the results their group has begun to obtain. As these figures do not seem to correspond with those that he had expected from his reading the night before, he checks quickly to see that Alexis is gainfully employed and then he has a quick consultation with the teacher. The teacher reassures James that this aberrant set of results is quite possible and suggests a couple of questions to fire back at the group. On his way back to the group, Alexis calls him over, and as he is James's first priority, he goes. He finds that the group has not progressed very far, so with a few prompts and an adjustment to the apparatus which he points out to the group, he is able to set them on a better path to gaining the results required. He then leaves them, returns to the group with the odd results and manages to make them think about the possible reasons for their different data. He checks the time and noting the approach of the end of the lesson, goes back to Alexis's group to make sure they can at least complete something worthwhile, and record a few results. When the teacher calls the class together, he again sits with Alexis's group and prompts its members to contribute to the discussion. When homework is given out, he records it in Alexis's diary for him, checking with Alexis that he understands what he has to do. He makes a few quick notes on the lesson plan about what had happened in the two groups he had particularly helped and gives it to the teacher as he leaves the laboratory with the pupils.

It does not always go smoothly. Sometimes the resources are not sufficient, time runs out or somebody's patience is not what it should be. Do not worry about this. Just remember what would have made it go better, and incorporate that next time you do that activity. We learn more from mistakes than doing things correctly.

Improve your practice

Watch teachers and others at work and see how they talk with pupils. With their permission, make notes of their body language, tone of voice, the sort of vocabulary they are using.

- What seems to work well?
- Did any of their behaviour seem inappropriate?

Share the notes with those whom you have watched. If they agree, share them with colleagues.

- Could you adapt any ideas that you see for yourself?

If you are really brave, get yourself videoed and watch what body language and verbal prompts you use. It takes practice, despite it looking very easy to an onlooker.

You should not be put in charge of a large group and certainly not a whole class at the level you are aiming for. If the group is meant to be working together cooperatively, you may need to ensure shy ones speak and other more vocal pupils do not dominate. Act like an informal chairperson. Some groups, however, may be meant to be working independently, so your role may be to stop the irrelevant chat to enable them to complete their tasks. Enabling pupils to cooperate and challenge each other is giving them a most valuable life skill [2-1.2:iii]. You might be the only adult in the room for a short emergency period, but you should be under the supervision of a qualified teacher at all times.

Feedback and record keeping

You need to monitor, even informally, how the pupils are progressing and what achievement they make in a lesson, then feed back to the teacher [2-3.2:6]. It can be verbal or on paper depending on your task and the teachers you are working with. Annotating a planning sheet is easy, or the Post-it on the planning sheet returned to the teacher is useful [2-3.1:5]. Ensure before your lesson you have arranged for some kind of information exchange after the lesson. Assessment information is best when gathered against the objective for the session, so it is doubly important that you know what this is. It would also be useful for the teacher to know how well the pupils are progressing towards their targets, particularly in literacy or from an IEP, as these are likely to be specific and short-term; also what their behaviour is like, especially if a behaviour programme is in place, and what unexpected things you noticed. Figure 7.2 shows TA comments on IEP objectives; it has had the pupil's name removed.

If no sheet has been provided then just note down anything significant you have observed on a Post-it or memo pad. This will help you remember what you want to say when talking to the teacher. This feedback may have to be informal; it can even be in the corridor as you walk away together, even the car park, or relaxing in the staffroom together. Try and keep feedback constructive [2-3.1:4]. It may be something about the pupils' performance [2-3.2:6], the suitability of the activity or a curriculum point about what has been learnt [2-5.1:4].

Sometimes you may be working with pupils regularly on your own, carrying out simple physiotherapy for instance. Keep a simple notebook as a diary and use it to jot down significant changes. If you are not sure what is significant, ask the teacher or therapist what to look out for.

Case study: Good practice in feedback

Jani, a TA, was trained by a visiting occupational therapist to work with two Year 1 pupils. One had dyspraxia, sometimes called 'clumsy child syndrome', and the other a mild form of cerebral palsy. He kept an exercise book just dating the changes in the way the children did the exercises. He kept a copy of the timetable and did the exercises daily. The teacher got him to liaise with the visiting therapist and after a couple of visits and discussions Jani found himself making minor adaptations to the exercises as the children seemed to progress, which he noted. He then checked with the class teacher and the therapist, both of whom were delighted with his initiative, yet responsible monitoring and reporting of the situation.

Remember, if you write anything, it should be accurate, concise, legible, dated and be kept in an appropriately confidential and secure place [2-1.2:1, 2 & 3].

You may be asked to complete more formal assessment sheets as part of your job. If this is so, do ensure you have complete instructions as to what you are to observe and what to write [2-3.1:6]. This may become evidence in a reporting process. Sometimes TAs who have worked closely with a pupil with special needs may be asked to write their own report of what they are doing, and how their charges have progressed (or not). Again, get full instructions about what is required, be brief, concise and accurate. If possible, get the document typed, but only by a member of the school staff. Always date any such record and sign it.

INDIVIDUAL EDUCATION PLAN & REVIEW

Name of pupil: ....   Date of plan: 16.11.01   Date of next plan: 02.02

Objectives/targets planned with parents and pupils

Long term objectives (across the curriculum)	Current level (from previous IEP progress)	Short-term objectives/targets and success criteria	DATE	DETAILS (including targets and date achieved in red pen)
Social and Behavioural	.... met this target and can work for 10 minutes when unsupervised by an adult once a day.	.... will be able to work unsupervised for 15 mins once per session.	14/3/02	Reading book: 1st book too hard, 2nd book too easy - talked about sharks! Spelling test. 15/20 - tried hard. 1-1 30 mins
Listening Skills	.... met this target and is now able to complete a task following a one-part instruction.	.... will be able to repeat back to giver, a two-part instruction and then complete the task with 50% accuracy.	18/3/02	Read book. Is sounding out well. Recognising Warwick words. LWL2. 39 words + 20 new = 59 word I picked out words he's been learning in Warwick - he knew them immediately. TB
Writing	.... met this target and is now forming his letters correctly. However his writing seldom has spaces between words.	.... will maintain the formation of his letters and be able to write sentences that have finger spaces between words with 75% success.	9/4/02	.... worked on no bonds 1-1 25 mins to 10 - very well. He was very enthusiastic. Spellings 9/10 reading 25/25 stickers given J.M.
Reading	New Target. .... can read all the words on Word List 1.	.... will learn to read 15 of the words on Word List 2 in any context.	11.4.02	Reading book. Warwick words. Read 22 cvc words and 25 (3+) at sight words (although a little hesitant, needs time) Counted 1>10 and back 1>15 and back not fully confident at this 1-1 10 m...
Maths	This was a partially achieved target. .... can work with bonds to and within 10 using addition but not consistently with subtraction.	.... will be able to recognise and use number bonds to 10 and within 10 using subtraction.	14.04.02	.... did not want to do the song 16.04.02 ...... but the column. He kept using the smallest no first so he got in a muddle practised no bonds to 10 100% with ruler + oots of days of week - Not yet known JM

Cc Parent/s/Carers ☐   SENCO ☐   Class Teacher/s ☐   Teaching Assistants ☐   Head of Year ☐   Other ☐   File ☐

Figure 7.2   An IEP with feedback by a TA

97

Using your initiative within the boundaries of your role

As you can see from the above, you may be given quite some leeway to interpret instructions, carry out activities, prepare materials and report back. Teachers usually appreciate having people to work with who have ideas, who ask questions, who are prepared to do things 'off their own bat'. But they will all vary as to the extent they are happy for you to do this. This is where your sensitivity must come in. You have to judge how far you can properly go in any situation in any classroom. What will help you is to talk it through whenever you can with the teacher, preferably beforehand, but if not make sure any unilateral action on your part is reported back to the teacher as part of your feedback.

One teacher may be very happy for you to give permission for a pupil to visit the toilet, and another insist all such permission is rarely given in their class, or certainly only by them. Use of certain materials not specified in the planning might need permission for use – or not. The whole issue of boundaries with each class teacher for whom you work has to be worked out between the pair of you. It really does help to be as explicit as possible about such boundaries. Written policies may help you, but many of the issues will be ones of individual idiosyncrasies and relationships.

8 Supporting the curriculum

The curriculum itself

Any task that you are given to do with pupils will not be just to occupy them, but will be designed to help them learn something. What actually goes on in the classroom for the pupil learner depends on the match between what the teacher wants them to learn – the curriculum; the learning style and characteristics of the pupil; and the activities of the adults teaching and supporting the learning.

A curriculum can mean a course of study at a school but really the word covers everything that goes on in school. The formal part, the part that is now written down, is what most people think of when they refer to a school curriculum. But much more is learnt when in school. You may remember things you learnt at school, that were not prescribed, about other pupils and teachers themselves, about how friendships work and how to keep out of trouble. These aspects are sometimes called the 'informal' or the 'hidden' curriculum. The informal curriculum covers the bits everybody knows goes on between lessons: in the corridors or the playground, assembly or clubs; and the hidden curriculum covers the bits about relationships and climate, the way you feel when you work or visit a place.

The formal curriculum

This covers what schools hope to teach. If you work in a state funded school, this includes the National Curriculum (NC) as a legal requirement in English and Welsh schools. Independent schools are free to set their own curriculum, although some follow the NC or parts of it. The NC is dictated by government, and is an entitlement for all children of statutory school age (5–16). Scotland has an advisory NC and Northern Ireland has its own version.

The National Curriculum

Making the curriculum a legal requirement means that everyone has a right to be taught certain subjects at certain ages, and it ensures there is a breadth and balance, coherence and consistency, relevance and differentiation. These long

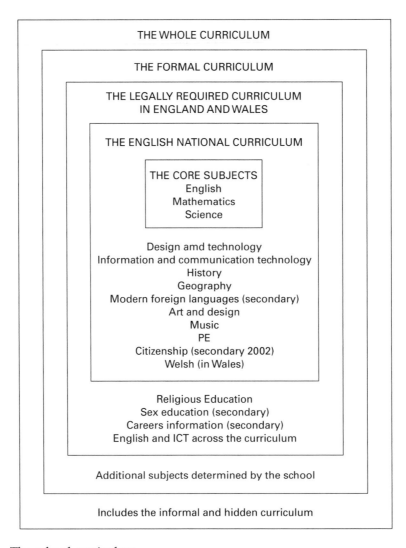

Figure 8.1 The school curriculum
© Source: Watkinson 2002: 17

words are all written into the legal descriptions of the NC. All schools will have copies of the documents and it is well worth reading the introductory pages (DfEE/QCA 1999a; DfEE/QCA 1999b: 10–13) on 'Values, aims and purposes', and the requirements made of schools and teachers including its structure and timing. The latest revision published to begin in September 2000 stated the aims of this NC as:

Aim 1: The school curriculum should aim to provide opportunities for all pupils to learn and to achieve . . .

Aim 2: The school curriculum should aim to promote pupils' spiritual, moral, social and cultural development and prepare all pupils for the opportunities, responsibilities and experiences of life . . .

The four main purposes of the National Curriculum: To establish an entitlement, to establish standards, to promote continuity and coherence and to promote public understanding.

(DfEE/QCA 1999a; DfEE/QCA 1999b: 13)

The original documents laid out the subjects of an NC that had to be studied in England: English, mathematics and science, which it denoted as the core, and the foundation subjects of design and technology, information technology (IT), art, music, PE, history and geography and after age 11 a modern foreign language. Religious education (RE) was included in a basic curriculum, and cross-curricular linked areas were described later. Welsh was made an additional subject for pupils in Wales. It aimed to challenge expectations and raise standards and broaden the range of subjects studied. Spiritual, moral, social and cultural education, citizenship and environmental education are now more closely defined by the new Curriculum 2000.

The original documentation looked daunting with a separate ring file for each subject. This did not matter so much in secondary schools, where each teacher is usually only responsible for one subject, but primary teachers have to teach them all except the modern language. This is now relatively slimmer, and we do not have legislation that insists on the same material being delivered in the same way at the same time on each day of the week, each week, month and year. We do not have standardised, centrally legislated and produced lesson texts from which we all work. Some countries do.

You may find the jargon of the NC hard, but it will help to understand a few technical terms.

The Foundation Stage

Children between three and five years old are said to be in the Foundation Stage. The aims of the Foundation Stage are to underpin all future learning by developing children's:

- personal, social and emotional well-being
- positive attitudes and dispositions towards their learning
- social skills
- attention skills and persistence
- language and communication
- reading and writing
- mathematics
- knowledge and understanding of the world
- physical development
- creative development.

Early Learning Goals define assessment levels for the teachers.

Other National Curriculum jargon

Four key stages give a structure of years running throughout the statutory school system. Year 1 contains those children who were five before the end of August. If they were in school before 1 September, they were either in a nursery class or a reception or foundation class.

- Key Stage 1 contains Years 1 and 2 (infants).
- Key Stage 2 contains Years 3 to 6 (juniors).
- Key Stage 3 contains Years 7 to 9.
- Key Stage 4 contains Years 10 and 11.
- Sixth forms, if they exist, will contain Years 12 and 13 (very occasionally referred to as Key Stage 5).

The compulsory levels of delivery for all the NC subjects are only Key Stages 1, 2 and 3.

General Certificates of Secondary Education (GCSEs) and General National Vocational Qualifications and their courses are for Key Stage 4.

Advanced level work ('A2' and 'AS' level) is usually done in sixth forms, tertiary colleges and further education (FE) colleges.

Programmes of Study describe what should be taught, the basis for planning and teaching.

Attainment targets provide a framework in a nine-level scale for assessment in eight levels and a level for exceptional performance. They set out the 'knowledge, skills and understanding that pupils of different abilities and maturities are expected to have by the end of each key stage' (Education Act 1996).

Level descriptions are defined for each level and describe the types and range of performance that pupils working at that level should show. They provide the basis for making judgements about pupils' performance at the end of Key Stages 1, 2 and 3, and so provide the basis for teachers to make their assessments.

Standard Assessment Tasks or Tests (SATs) are based on level descriptions.

Schemes of work should be drawn up by each school for each subject. They show in which year particular parts of the NC will be taught in your school, the resources available and probably lots of ideas for activities.

The **Qualifications and Curriculum Authority (QCA)** has produced model schemes of work for schools, to save them reinventing the wheel, and while many schools have adopted them, they are not a legal requirement.

A **syllabus** is even more detailed than a scheme of work, and sets out exactly what should be covered. These can be drawn up by schools themselves, based on the NC or on the syllabuses devised by the examination boards for the external examinations.

The **Office for Standards in Education (Ofsted)** inspects schools using published guidance. This includes specific criteria against which the school is measured, which include the way in which the NC is planned, delivered by teachers and support staff, received by pupils and the learning outcomes.

Curriculum 2000

The aims of Curriculum 2000 are 'to provide opportunities for all pupils to learn and to achieve . . . to promote pupils' spiritual, moral, social and cultural development and prepare all pupils for the opportunities, responsibilities and experiences of life' (DfEE/QCA 1999a; DfEE/QCA 1999b: 12) and are based on a statement of values about the self, relationships, society and the environment (pp. 148, 149).

Curriculum 2000 provided an inclusive framework aiming that:

The learning across the curriculum should promote:

- spiritual, moral, social and cultural development
- personal, social and health education and citizenship
- skills development
- financial capability, enterprise education and education for sustainable development.

It also said that:

Teachers, when planning, should adapt or modify teaching and/or learning approaches and materials to provide all pupils with opportunities to succeed:

- Setting appropriate challenges
- Providing for the diversity of pupils' needs
- Providing for pupils with special educational needs
- Providing support for pupils for whom English is an additional language.

Since the beginning of the NC, IT has become information and communication technology (ICT) and now includes using the Internet. ICT and RE became designated as part of the legally required core for all children, although English, mathematics and science are still called the 'core subjects'. RE documents are not included within the main set of NC books, but are published as a 'locally agreed syllabus'. All community and voluntary controlled schools in England and Wales have to use these. Foundation and aided schools can make their own decisions, but have to have an agreed syllabus of some kind. Guidelines for teaching citizenship along with personal, social and health education (PSHE) became part of the NC documentation.

Each subject in the NC is set out in the same way; each has a different colour. As they are now all in one document for either primary or secondary, you would find it useful to obtain a copy for yourself. If you are in a middle school, you may need to refer to both. Some subjects only have one part to them but English, mathematics and science all have separate parts – each with different attainment targets. You need not read and learn these in detail, just refer to them when they are relevant or you are particularly interested. The colour codes are:

- English: orangey-yellow
- mathematics: deep blue
- science: scarlet red
- design and technology: green

- ICT: plummy red
- history: purple
- geography: brown
- art and design: orange
- music: pink
- PE: pale blue
- PSHE, citizenship, environmental education and modern languages: white

The stages by which an average pupil is expected to reach each level are:

- End of Year 1: level 1
- End of Year 2: level 2
- End of Year 4: level 3
- End of Year 6: level 4
- End of Year 9: level 5
- End of Year 11: level 6

Brighter children reach the levels earlier, and slower learners spend a longer time getting to each level.

The Literacy and Numeracy Strategies

Alongside the definitions in the NC of what must be taught have recently come the twin strategies for literacy and numeracy. Many of you may now be employed to work in specially supporting pupils in these areas. English includes literacy – reading and writing – but it also includes speaking and listening. For some of the younger children whom you may be working with, this area is so difficult for them that they will need help with it before they will be able to read and write with any understanding. The National Literacy Strategy (NLS) (DfEE 1998c) was introduced into primary schools in 1998, and the National Numeracy Strategy (NNS) (DfEE 1999c) in 1999. For some of you, working with the strategies involves the use of specially written materials, such as Additional Literacy Support (ALS). These materials are usually introduced with specific training and are well covered in the DfES and DfEE Induction training modules. If you are not able to attend any of these sessions, do ask what training you can attend as some of the requirements of the programmes are quite technical. The year 2000–1 piloted the introduction of the strategies to Key Stage 3, and TAs are now working with materials especially written for them for English and mathematics in Year 7 and in Year 1 which is sometimes called Early Literacy Support (ELS). Some of the catch-up programmes and materials used for booster classes are also available in schools, but you will be given directions for all these materials.

The strategies have resulted in a much more formal approach to the subjects, with suggested structure to lessons, and in the case of literacy even recommended times to be taken over each part of the lesson. It is still all up to the discretion of the school to determine the way in which these strategies are used in other subjects, additional experiences beyond those set out, the style of resources used and the time of day that these subjects take place. Much more didactic class teaching has resulted, and some of you may find your role during that class teaching time becomes questionable. Do try to attend any staff meetings associated with the strategies, and get a copy of the handbooks for yourselves.

A down side of the strategies, which have been very successful in creating consistency in planning and teaching in schools, is that in some schools too much time has been spent on literacy and numeracy, squeezing out the other subjects. The idea of a broad and balanced curriculum, accessible to all, enabling all children to experience success, has not yet been realised for some pupils but it is possible (Ofsted 2002). The withdrawal of groups for specific support can have implications for inclusion, although the children usually enjoy the activities. It is possible that a child receiving specific support in Year 1 may need support throughout their school career exposing them to a constant diet of being boosted and depriving them of other experiences. Hard decisions have to be made by schools and parents.

Other aspects of the curriculum

The formal curriculum

Schools have to have policies for sex education and behaviour management and can set out anything else they want to teach in their prospectuses. If you have got a copy of the prospectus for the school in which you are working, have a look at what they say about their curriculum. They are also supposed to set out how they intend to teach this formal curriculum. Some books talk about 'delivering' the curriculum, but it is probably clear to you, to use the old saying, 'You can take a horse to water but you cannot make it drink.' Delivery alone is not enough, the contents have to be understood and used. We must also recognise the importance of individual achievements, and the value of encouraging pupils to want to learn, to value themselves and of stimulating curiosity and creativity. A challenging task!

Each school will have its own curriculum policies, laying down how each subject is to be taught, resourced and assessed in that school [2-5.1:i]. If you are regularly helping in particular lessons you need to obtain a copy of the relevant policy and see how your presence fits in with what the school wishes to achieve [2-5.2:i]. Try to attend the staff meetings associated with that subject. If you are in a secondary school, it may well be advisable to consider taking a GCSE in the subject if you do not already have one. This is especially true of science and geography where the technical language is specific to the subject and can be the source of confusion for the student. You need to be sure of your own facts and skills before you can help others. You need to be able not only to read worksheets but to interpret them for students with learning problems; you need to be able to show students how to use apparatus safely and accurately. This goes from using rulers through to complicated specialist equipment. You need to know when accuracy matters or numbers of results. It is hoped that all TAs have

GCSE or its equivalent in mathematics and English or are in the process of attaining them, in order to be able to help pupils adequately and accurately, as numeracy and literacy underpin recording and communicating information in all other subjects.

The informal curriculum

Because the informal curriculum is not set out in legal requirements, every school will be different in what it expects of this area. As a TA, you may well be involved in helping run one of the clubs or caring for one of the areas outside the classrooms. You need to know how it fits in the scheme of things for your school. Outside, all schools have some kind of play area for break-times and most have some kind of grounds. Some schools still have to walk or even bus their pupils to their playing fields and not all of those are in urban areas. For those who have grounds, part of their informal curriculum will include how they want those grounds used and maintained, and some have even developed outside classrooms. Environmental areas, with ponds and wildlife bits, need caring for. As it is likely that you are a more local person to the school than many of the teachers, you may well get involved in helping look after outside study areas. Some TAs have set up such areas as projects for higher TA qualifications.

The hidden curriculum

Things that used to be implicit in the way schools worked are becoming more and more explicit, so less is 'hidden'. Things like politeness and care of property used to be taken for granted, but now sometimes have to be part of the explicit behaviour policy. Treating everybody with courtesy, whatever their needs, colour, creed or race, is spelt out in equal opportunities and anti-discrimination policies. An Ofsted inspection of a school recognises these less definable areas.

> Among other things: Inspectors must evaluate and report on:
> . . . extra-curricular activities . . .
> . . . a broad range of worthwhile opportunities . . .
> . . . is socially inclusive . . . pupils . . . develop an understanding of living in a community;
> . . . the steps taken to ensure pupils' welfare, health and safety, including the school's arrangements for child protection . . . the school has effective measures . . . to eliminate oppressive behaviour including all forms of harassment and bullying.
>
> (Ofsted 1999: 38)

You know when visiting schools, maybe on your first visit to the school you are now working in, that schools have a climate. They try to define this in words, describing their 'ethos', but it is hard to legislate for happiness. While 'to be a happy place' cannot be the first aim of a school (we could say that about homes or social clubs), pupils will not learn if they are unhappy and staff will not work with a will if they are miserable. Once you are a member of staff you will also be part of that school and a little responsible for its climate. Respect and support are needed by you, but you will have your part to play to give it to all the other staff as well as the pupils.

Freiberg and Stein (1999) said:

> School climate is the heart and soul of a school. It is about that essence of a school that leads a child, a teacher, an administrator, a staff member to love the school and look forward to being there each day. School climate is about that quality of a school that helps each person feel personal worth, dignity and importance while simultaneously helping create a sense of belonging to something beyond ourselves. The climate of a school can foster resilience or become a risk factor in the lives of people who work and learn in a place called school.

(p. 11)

Your relationships, spelt out in Chapter 3, taking responsibility for your own actions, and the actions of others with pupils as well as staff all contribute to this hidden curriculum.

Supporting specific subjects in the curriculum is given in more detail in the following two chapters.

9 Supporting literacy and numeracy

Supporting English

Developing literate pupils

Your role in supporting pupils is crucial. Mastery of the skills of English is essential for pupils if they are to succeed in other curriculum areas. TAs commonly help with English skills in the primary school literacy hour which followed the directions of the NLS. The hour is organised into three parts: a whole class teaching time, a period for group work and a feedback or plenary time. Such were the demands made upon teachers for purposeful group work that many schools redirected their existing TA workforce or appointed new TAs to work with teachers during this time. Classes became timetabled and TAs matched to fit these timetables in order to staff the groups as fully as possible. This pattern of the three-part lesson is becoming more common in secondary schools where the Key Stage 3 strategy has taken hold. In practice, good teachers always had a shape to their lessons, but the NLS suggested a much more rigid compartmentalising of the time than most teachers were used to.

Specific training for TAs to support particular groups of pupils whose test results had shown them to be under the expected levels for their ages was introduced and many TAs will have been on the training that accompanied the publication of the materials. This material is referred to as the ALS (DfEE 1999d). This book does not intend to cover the use of this material, or the demands of the NLS in any great detail, as this requires specific training. Your school should induct you properly into its use. Fox and Halliwell's book (2000) will also be of some use in this area.

Secondary TAs are most likely to be employed to support pupils who have SEN in the area of English work, causing them problems in all lessons. Pupils who managed in a more flexible primary school regime find secondary teacher expectations of use of correct vocabulary, reading textbooks and worksheets, note-taking in class and written homework more demanding. Gaps between those who are fluent and the less able become wider as pupils get older. Help may become more specifically linguistic in lessons other than English. Liaison with individual teachers and the SENCO is vital to understand the nature of your tasks and their purpose. It is possibly even more important to take note of the effect of your help on a pupil, how support can label, possibly causing some victimisation, or the pupil finds attention irksome. If there is any such problem you must discuss it with the pupil's tutor, your line manager or the SENCO.

English as an additional language

The pupils may not be native English speakers and so English is not their main language but an additional language (EAL) [2-5.1:viii]. Helping such pupils may also need some specialist tuition, so enquire from your mentor or line manager if you feel you need extra support. If you work with children who have English as an additional language then you will work with them in ways that are very similar to the support you provide for others; however, such children have some very specific needs which you will need to think about. Most EAL children will not have SEN needs just as you would not suddenly have SEN if you went to live in Japan. Their problem is having to learn in a language that is new to them.

It is important that you learn to pronounce their name correctly; have access to books or tapes in the pupil's home language; learn a few words in their language (things like 'good morning', 'hello' and 'welcome' are always useful). The children will respond positively to visual prompts to help explain an activity so keep a look out for pictures that would help explain activities. If they make an error in spoken English then do not correct it. Simply provide a correct model (just as you did with your own children when they were learning to talk).

The children may need help in understanding any key vocabulary and this would be an excellent place to start in supporting them. They may have particular problems with idiom; many EAL children take things literally. What are they thinking if they hear someone say, 'I'll murder him before he gets much older'?

The English policy

The English coordinator or head of English should be able to give you a copy of the school's policy document and/or scheme of work [2-5.1:i & v]. As you read it you will begin to understand the school's priorities for English. **It is particularly important that you know the value of speaking and listening as a tool for delivering work in literacy as this may not be made clear from the objectives you have been given.**

All strands of English are important and are interrelated. The first to develop is talk and this is a key tool for learning. Children develop their understandings of texts through talk. Questions to encourage this are important. If you ask, 'Where did Goldilocks go?' the answer is liable to be quite literal. If, however, the question had been, 'Should Goldilocks have gone into the cottage?' or 'Would you do what Goldilocks did?' the answers would help with a deeper understanding of the text. Children who have problems reading and writing often show real understanding when given the opportunity to discuss. It is likely that the teacher will provide key questions for you. It is also all right to supplement these with your own once you know how the session is going.

Children develop the skills of reading and writing at the same time [2-5.1:ii & vi]. The teacher may well ask you to work on a specific strand where the child needs extra help. It is always useful to remember how closely these strands are related. When teaching phonics you can help children with skills that are useful for both reading and writing as Figure 9.1 shows.

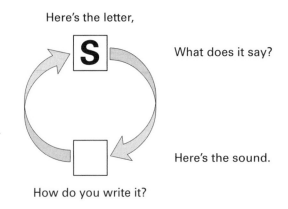

Figure 9.1 The phonic circle

Work on phonics therefore can, and should, support reading and writing. Useful resources to look for in school are:

- *Progression in phonics (PIPS)* (DfEE 1999e)
- *Developing Early Writing* (DfES 2001c)
- *The Spelling Bank* (DfEE 1999f)
- *Additional Literacy Support (ALS) materials* (DfEE 1999d)

Learning problems in English

You should be informed if there is a specific learning problem and be given a chance to discuss it with the SENCO [2-5.1:iii]. However, there can be instances when a pupil has a problem not related to the long-term one. An example of this would be an ear infection which could mean that a pupil is not hearing clearly. Another example would be where the pupil you are working with has been involved in some kind of emotional upheaval and this too can have an adverse effect on learning.

When dealing with specific problems then you should be able to see the pupil's IEP [2-5.1:iv]. This will deal with the specific areas the pupil needs to work on and will give a measure of past targets met. The areas may be general or very specific. One instance of the latter might be that you would work with a pupil with poor spelling skills when other areas of learning present no problem.

Pupils have three main learning styles which clearly affect their English learning [2-5.1:ii]. They can be visual, auditory or kinaesthetic (VAK) learners. The needs of each group of learners are different and specific. Although some pupils may exhibit strong preferences for one learning style, others will be a mixture. Some important features are outlined below.

Visual learners put information in a visual form like graphs or pictures. They often write things down to help them remember. They would rather watch than act or talk and are more likely to remember what they see. They can be quiet by nature and have difficulty concentrating during verbal activities. They are usually very well organised, like to read, can be good spellers and like detail. They look upwards when trying to remember.

Auditory learners remember best what they hear and say. They very often talk aloud therefore it is very important for them to talk through new learning. They enjoy class discussions. They whisper when reading 'silently'. When learning to spell they need to hear the rhythm and sound of the letters. They do not need to look at you to hear you. When trying to recall information they will often cock the head to one side.

Kinaesthetic learners remember what they do and experience. They like to find ways to move around as they work through problems. They cannot sit still for long and this means that they need regular breaks. They will often tap their feet or pencils and seem to be always fiddling with something. These learners are often outgoing by nature and lose interest when not actively involved. They can be poor spellers. When talking to people they will often touch them. They like physical rewards.

For all the reasons outlined above it is necessary for pupils to experience interactive activities that meet the needs of each of the learners. Talk, investigations, drama, sorting, sequencing and drawing are just a few techniques that help in this area. It would be worth while just watching the children you work with and seeing which type of activities they respond to with most enthusiasm and where they have most fun. How many of the characteristics mentioned above do they have? After all, no one would suggest that learning should be dull and yet for some pupils that is just what it has become [2-5.1:vii].

The literacy lesson

During a literacy lesson, you will work with pupils in a variety of ways. There should be a clear learning objective in the teacher's planning for any part of the hour when you will be working with children, either individually or on their own. For any session, the activity should be clearly outlined and the teacher may have collected the resources for you [2-5.2:1]. There may well be some indication of where you are expected to be working and of any other necessary information, e.g. will your group be expected to share in the plenary? This information is important as it gives you and your group an opportunity to prepare and rehearse for the plenary thus ensuring success. Many teachers leave space on this sheet for your evaluations of the activity and assessment information you consider important. Figures 9.2 to 9.5 shown below may be useful.

One of the criticisms levelled at the use of TAs in the formal teacher instruction part of the lesson is that they are wasting their time. It is important that you and the teacher are clear what the purpose of your presence is at this time.

| What I want the children to learn. |
| Description of the activity. |
| Resources needed. |
| Where the work is to be recorded. |
| Evaluation of the session. |
| Important assessment information. |

Figure 9.2 Planning for literacy (1)
© Source: Margaret Bickmore

| Objective |
| Task |
| Evaluation |

Figure 9.3 Planning for literacy (2)
© Source: Margaret Bickmore

What I want the children to learn.	What evidence is there that such learning has occurred?
Activity:	
Key questions	How did the children respond to the questions?
Resources needed	Assessment jottings

Figure 9.4 Planning for literacy (3)
© Source: Margaret Bickmore

| Children |
| Objective/what I want the children to learn |
| Resources required, including those for recording |
| Possible problems to look out for |
| Key questions |
| Assessment for this session |

Figure 9.5 Planning for literacy (4)
© Source: Margaret Bickmore

It could be:

- To observe a particular pupil or group of pupils, to see whether they are responding to the input from the teacher, how attentive they are, if they are asking or answering questions, what interests them or not. This can be done as a formal observation tick sheet or less formally.
- To ensure a particular group or individual remains part of the whole class by checking inappropriate behaviour or prompting pupils to question or answer when you know they can, or following a text with a separate copy and a finger under each word as the teacher reads. Visually impaired pupils may need specially made copies, and hearing impaired pupils may need signing interpretation.
- To take notes yourself of the lesson content, although this should be covered by your induction training and liaison with the teacher over planning.
- To role model sitting quietly and joining in the discussion.

The same applies to the plenary session. The main part of your work will be with groups or individuals during the middle part of the lesson.

Scope of learning objectives in the English/literacy standard [2-5.1]

a. To learn to read fluently and with confidence and understanding
Fluency comes through having real audiences and purposes for reading. It also grows out of an understanding of how texts work. It may be possible to prepare a reading with your group for sharing in the plenary or assembly. Another useful technique is to prepare a reading as if it were a play. One group or pupil reads the narrative link (you could do this if it is complicated or if there are only two of you). The others read what the characters say with appropriate expression.

As children become more fluent then their confidence increases. Confidence is also helped if the pupils are clear in their understanding of what the text is about. The latter is best accessed through discussion or drama. Pupils really enjoy talking in role. They could have the conversation between Goldilocks and Baby Bear, or between Little Bear and his best friend. Another useful technique is hot seating. In this either you or a pupil takes on the role of a character from a story and is questioned by the others. Think about using conscience alley. Here the pupils provide the voice of the character's conscience when they try to decide on a course of action.

b. To identify and explain key points and ideas in written materials
Pupils can do a range of things to help develop understanding in this area. Text marking is very useful. To do this pupils have a copy of the text. They might underline in red words to show you a character was angry, in blue words to show you what he did and green the consequences. Questioning will also help in this area, as will drama.

c. To develop legible handwriting
This may be within the literacy hour or outside it. Help the pupils, make sure of the following:

- They hold the pencil correctly.
- The pencil should be sharp.
- They should not hold the pencil too tightly.
- They need to know the correct letter formation.
- Their posture should be comfortable.
- They have paper at the correct angle.

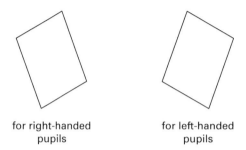

for right-handed
pupils

for left-handed
pupils

Figure 9.6   Angles of paper for writing

- Letters need to be formed correctly.
- The pen or pencil should be lifted from the paper as little as possible.
- When you write for them make sure your handwriting is in the school style and presents a good model.

d. To structure and organise written work
This is an area where pupils have a great many problems. They need to be able to plan for writing. This is not as easy as it seems. Different pupils will find different ways of planning more successful. The plans can be written, spoken or drawn using a range of formats.

Pupils will not be able to write well unless they have a clear picture of how this text type is organised. From the shared session with the teacher they will have a clearer idea of what is required. Help them to expand and revise this with you before they start. They should have a clear picture of what will make this piece of writing successful. Display this as they write so that they can access it. They need the confidence to have a go and to understand that mistakes are positive. It is from our mistakes that we learn. If you have to model or share write with a group then make mistakes, show them the thinking you go through to recognise them and the strategies you use to improve your work.

They need to rehearse each sentence before they write it. For younger children and auditory learners this is most successful done aloud. For others the rehearsal can be internal. They need to be able to find their own mistakes and to know how to correct them.

The development of writing stamina is important. Wrists and fingers do get tired so allow for the chance to stretch the fingers and flex them regularly.

e. To understand the sound and spelling system and use this to read and spell accurately
The teaching of phonics is very important. You will need to help children hear individual sounds, called 'phonemes'. It is very important that you say the

sounds correctly yourself. There is a tendency for people to put an 'uh' sound on the end of phonemes. Try to make sure you do *not* do this, or reduce it as much as you can. The following sounds should be pronounced as continuing sounds:

fff, lll, mmm, nnn, sss, shshsh

Children, once they can hear, say and write individual phonemes, need to be able to differentiate them in words. A range of activities can help here, such as:

Sound buttons
This involves placing a dot under each individual sound you hear in a word:

b l a ck
• •• •

Make sure you have sorted this out clearly in your own mind as it is no longer as we were taught. Once the initial three letters in 'spring' would have been the blend 'spr'. Now we expect the pupils to hear the sounds individually:

s p r i ng
•• •• •

The ALS and PIPS materials (produced by the DfES and available in schools) suggest a number of games which can be played by children thus helping develop their phonic awareness in a way that helps and is fun. One of the suggestions is:

Full Circle
To play this plastic letters are very useful. A word is put out. The children in the group listen in turn as a new word is said and change the one phoneme they need to. The letters pass around the circle until you get back to the first word (see Figure 9.7).

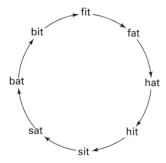

Figure 9.7   The word circle

Children will hear the beginning of a word first, followed by the end sound and then the middle. They find consonants easier to hear than vowels. There are some sounds that they muddle. A prime example of this is *t* and *d*.

Phonics for spelling is challenging for all. One of the main problems children face with our spelling system is the number of ways it is possible to spell a single sound. Just think of the long 'a' sound. We can spell it:

Pl**ay**
Th**ey**
M**a**t**e**
Eight
St**ai**n

to name but a few. In cases like these children need to know what the choices are and to have a system for working out the most appropriate choice.

- Do not spell the word for a pupil when he or she asks, instead help them to hear the phonemes and have a go. Then show them how close they were. Techniques like this make children believe they can write.
- When the pupil has finished writing, ask him or her to ring a few words that are misspelt. Show how close they were.
- Help the pupil think of similar words to help with spellings so that if I can spell 'light' I should be able to spell 'tight'.
- When writing for the pupil (as a scribe), make a mistake, show your uncertainty, try another way and get them to help you select the one that looks correct.

---

f. To listen with attention and understanding
The problem is ascertaining that children have listened. To ensure this, the most common way is to question them to find out what they have remembered. There are other powerful techniques you can use.

In pairs they can explain what they know about a subject, then they can report back to the group about what they have heard.

Listening triangles are another useful tool. Put the children into threes. Two of them discuss a subject while the third listens, makes notes and reports back.

If you are working with a larger group then two of them can research a topic. The next step is to get together with another pair and share what you have learnt. Decide as a foursome what you want to share with the whole group, or with the class in the plenary.

g. To contribute to discussions and take part in conversations
The smaller the group, the more confident children feel when sharing. In that respect they are no different to adults. If a dominant child is taking over the discussion then you could run it like circle time where you can only talk if you are holding a particular object. Talk partners is a very good way to involve every-one. It works really well if at the end each pair tell the others some main ideas discussed or decided upon. This is great for you as it is more manageable in a smaller group. You could organise discussions so that everyone takes their turn.

Supporting mathematics

Developing numerate pupils

In providing a superb document (*The National Numeracy Strategy*, DfEE 1999c) to assist with the teaching and learning of mathematics, Anita Straker and her team used a different word to that of the NC, which was mathematics, i.e. numeracy. Clearly numeracy has its roots in 'number' and 'numerate'. What is a numerate person? According to the dictionary a numerate person is familiar with the basic principles of mathematics therefore being familiar with more than the four rules of number (addition, subtraction, multiplication and division) but also conversant with algebra, shape and space, and data handling. On this basis numeracy includes more than just number work and as you look in the NNS documents you will see that they cover all the mathematics that a student is expected to study from reception to Year 9. Aplin's book (1998) is useful to support your work in numeracy.

Mathematics is essentially a practical subject and as such should involve pupils in using practical apparatus and enjoying problem-solving activities. If you consider how you yourself learn best you may well find that you learn most by doing or by watching or reading or by listening. Much valuable work has been done to identify ways in which we learn and VAK, which stands for visual (seeing), auditory (hearing) and kinaesthetic (doing), is already explained in the previous section on literacy. Learning should involve a range of activities with one approach not having preference over the others. The NNS promotes VAK learning and also adopts a cyclic approach to the study of mathematics. That is any topic, e.g. fractions, will be studied several times during a key stage, not just once which was the case in many schools previously. In this way learning is revised and reinforced and extended on a regular basis [2-5.2:ii].

The mathematics/numeracy policy

Schools will have their own policies for teaching and learning mathematics and numeracy, now ususally including the use of the NNS [2-5.2:i]. TAs may not have themselves got any qualifications in mathematics; traditionally it has been a subject about which people say, 'I hated maths at school' or 'I never could do maths.' If this is the case, you really should seriously consider going to an FE or AE college and taking a course in GCSE mathematics. Mathematics has changed over the years, and styles and methods of teaching with it. In order to understand the scope of the learning objectives mentioned in the NOS (LGNTO 2001: 23), you need to be fully aware of the developments that have taken place within mathematics over recent years.

- TAs operating in Key Stage 1 need a working knowledge of the Key Stage 1 and Key Stage 2 NNS.
- TAs working within Key Stage 2 need to be fully conversant with techniques present in Key Stage 1, Key Stage 2 and some of Key Stage 3.

- TAs working within Key Stage 3 need knowledge not just of Years 7–9 but at least the work techniques associated with Years 4, 5 and 6.
- All TAs working in mathematics classrooms need to be able to use and understand the range of methods, both mental and written used within their particular school [2-5.2:iii].

Talk with the mathematics coordinator or the head of mathematics as to the best way of understanding. It means that you need to be aware of the use of:

- **Two ways of carrying out addition of two-digit numbers**

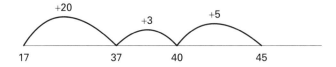

two ways of carrying out the addition 17 + 28

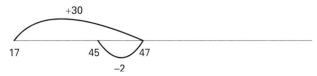

Figure 9.8 Adding two-digit numbers

- **blank number lines** to assist with addition and subtraction
- **multiplying two-digit numbers**

17 × 28

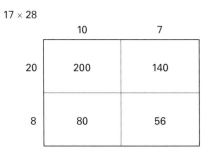

200 + 140 + 80 + 56 = 476

Figure 9.9 The grid method of multiplication

(For further examples see Numeracy Strategy Folder, Reception to Year 6 supplements of examples.)
- **the grid method for multiplication**
(Further examples can be seen in both the Reception to Year 6, and Years 7, 8 and 9 Numeracy Strategy Folders.)
- **chunking for division**
94 divided by 4
start with a known fact from the 4 times table
$10 \times 4 = 40$
so $20 \times 4 = 80$ (any more and we will be above 94) $94 - 80 = 14$

$1 \times 4 = 4$

$2 \times 4 = 8$

$3 \times 4 = 12$ (any more and we will be above 14) $14 - 12 = 2$

there must be $20 + 3$ lots of 4 in 94 with 2 remainder

so 94 divided by 4 is 23 remainder 2

(Further examples can be found in the supplements of example sections of the Numeracy Strategy documents.)

- **partitioning**: splitting numbers into constituent parts

$38 = 30 + 8$

$2756 = 2000 + 700 + 50 + 6$

It could also be $28 = 25 + 3$ depending on the calculation to be employed.

You need to use the methods appropriate to the stage of development of the pupils with whom you are working; you should not resort to methods you yourself learnt at school [2-5.2:v]. All appropriate methods are outlined in the NNS handbooks. Each class teacher has one; many TAs have their own but, at worst, you should have ready access to a copy within the establishment. Two other books produced by the NNS are useful, these being *Teaching mental calculation strategies* (QCA 1999a) and *Teaching written calculations* (QCA 1999b). It is inexcusable not to be able to use the methods, formal or informal, currently being employed with the class.

Vital to the success of the TA is the correct use of language and vocabulary. An excellent publication, the NNS Mathematical vocabulary book (DfEE 1999g), lists the majority of the vocabulary the pupils need; it is age/stage related and new words are highlighted within the text. Pages 4, 5 and 6 of this vocabulary book should be essential reading for any adult working within a mathematics lesson. These three pages cover the different types of questions (open, closed etc.) and give examples to assist the TA. Page 6 also provides sample questions to enable the TA to take the pupil on when they are 'stuck'. A publication *Handbook for Leading Mathematics Teachers* (DfEE 2000d) takes discussion on use of questions further, looking at prompting, probing and promoting questions.

Many schools involve TAs in the delivery of catch-up programmes such as Springboard 4, Springboard 7 etc. It is beyond the scope of this chapter to look at the range of ways the TA can assist or should assist in the delivery of such programmes. Each school has their own views on these intervention programmes and must use them in the best way they see fit.

The daily mathematics lesson

The three-part daily mathematics lesson (DML) is now firmly established within the primary phase and is becoming increasingly common within Key Stage 3. There is no doubt that effective use of TA support in Key Stages 1 and 2 has contributed greatly to the recent improvements in Level 4 scores and the increased enjoyment of and popularity of maths with primary-age pupils [2-5.2:vii]. Unfortunately, deployment of TAs within mathematics lessons is variable and what follows, while being the norm for some, will represent an ideal for others.

While some TAs may be contracted to work with specific pupils [2-5.2:iv], nevertheless they should take note of all aspects of this model as issues of inclusion and entitlement arise for all pupils within a class.

Oral and mental starter (OMS)
This is by far the most popular and effective part of the lesson. Dependent upon the age of the pupils and available space (Key Stages 1 and 2) the OMS either takes place with the pupils sitting at their desks or grouped together on the floor (carpet time). Within the OMS, you should work primarily with those pupils needing greatest support. Model with these pupils the activity being run by the teacher. You need to have any resources needed readily to hand [2-5.2:vi] such as

- **White boards and marker pens**: a superb resource. All children in the group write their response to a question on the board and then show the adult their answer at the same time. This means that all can be involved without any 'fear factor'. Communication is between the individual and the leader of the task. This is also useful for children working in pairs.
- **Number cards** either used singly or in pairs are very useful for pace value work, e.g. 'Find the digits 3, 5, 7'; 'Show me the biggest three-digit number you can make'. Children hold up their answers and the teacher can assess the answers extremely quickly.
- **Hundred squares** are a vital aid to children's understanding of the number system, to aid the processes of addition and subtraction mentally and the ability to count on in steps of different sizes.
- **Calculators:** used as an aid for learning calculators can be invaluable. The constant facility is extremely useful. Try this sequence of button presses:
  $5 + + = 0$
  Now press = five times.
  What happens to the display?
  (It should show 5, 10, 15, 20, 25. In other words you have created a machine to count in 5s.)
  Ask the children what number you will get to if you press = three more times
  Do it to check.
  Other questions such as 'How many presses to 100?', 'Will the display ever show 47?' can be helpful to a child's development with table knowledge.
- **Counters** such as cubes, rulers, number lines, dice and money are all useful items to have around when working with groups of children, particularly the younger ones or the less able older ones. These will enable you to engage and support these pupils with the activity.

Careful and appropriate use of language, correct mathematical vocabulary and questions should enable you to involve pupils fully in the OMS. Such involvement greatly assists the teacher in maintaining pace and in providing a brisk, interactive and meaningful start to the lesson.

Where the best OMSs take place, the interaction between the teacher and TA is seamless – a nod, a raised hand, a cough or some such gesture from you alerts the teacher that a member of your group has an answer or suitable contribution to make, thus enabling the teacher to involve pupils fully from your group. Arrange some sort of signal when you are planning together. The sense of achievement that such careful and sensitive involvement creates in pupils with learning difficulties is immeasurable.

An interesting observation of OMSs, where pupils sit on the carpet, is that the TA usually sits at the back of the group with her cohort of less able pupils; other pupils who may not always be that confident tend to gravitate towards the TA, dipping in and out of her support as and when necessary. This is a bonus to the class teacher as it can sort out potential later difficulties before they happen. This also prevents the distinctive 'labelling' of pupils. All the class see you as a resource to be used. It is important that the support is confidence-building or strategy-giving, not doing the work for the pupils by giving the answers.

In some instances the class teacher may ask the TA to work in an observational manner, for example 'Today in the oral and mental starter I want you to keep a record of who answers the questions' or 'I want you to keep track of a particular group or cohort of pupils and make notes on how they work together on this problem.' This is of course a valid use of the TA's time as it assists the teacher with the assessment process.

The plenary

One of the main purposes of the plenary is that it provides the teacher with opportunity to assess the learning that has taken place during the lesson. A good question and answer session based upon predetermined issues should give the teacher necessary information to assist with next steps planning. TA support in the plenary should mirror that which is given in the OMS. You will enable the less able pupils to fully participate [2-5.2:iv]. You should, by use of questions and prompts, help these children to cement the learning of the lesson, to firm up their ideas and to help cancel out any misconceptions that have arisen during the work part of the main teaching activity. You will, by the nature of the plenary, be assisting the teacher in the informal assessment of the understanding of the group as a whole.

Good use of language, questions and vocabulary are again vital and you should have access to any resources necessary to assist with the pupils' involvement in the plenary, for example any of the items of equipment mentioned for use in the OMS, plus blank paper for jottings and vocabulary cards to assist the children with formulating answers using the correct words. Remember, pages 4 to 6 from the vocabulary book (DfEE 1999g) can be helpful to you in formulating and asking the 'best' sort of questions to support the pupils' learning and participation.

The main part of the lesson

Many TAs will recognise their own practice in the previous two sections, indeed most lessons mirror the model outlined above. Where there is most variance in practice is the main part of the three-part lesson.

In lessons with a substantial teaching element, that is where a new topic is being introduced, you should sit with and assist the less able group of pupils modelling for them the teaching being delivered. You need to have any appropriate equipment or resources to hand and to have been briefed prior to the lesson. Once the direct teaching part of this type of lesson is complete and the pupils are engaged upon some other activity (written or other) in a first lesson on a topic you should remain as direct support for these pupils. In this way there is a significant support structure in place for those very pupils who need most support when learning new concepts or skills. In all main parts of lessons where direct teaching is taking place the TA should assist the least able pupils.

If the lesson is a follow-up lesson or a consolidation lesson, with minimal input from the teacher at the start of the second phase of the lesson, you need not and should not be restricted to working with the less able pupils. There is a requirement that the class teacher works with all pupils within a class and this means that the teacher has to spend at least one of the week's mathematics lessons working more closely with the least able pupils. During such occasions the TA should operate with other groups including the most able. On occasions you could even hold a watching brief over two groups, thus providing less intensive support but monitoring and intervening as and when appropriate.

During each week all pupils need time to work unaided, as they need to develop as independent learners. There are exceptions to every rule and if you have a contract to support a particular pupil, it will inevitably skew the role towards the group containing the particular pupil, but you can operate a watching brief over the target group providing necessary opportunities for independent work.

Mathematics resources

A very useful device for the TA to have is their own maths resource box. You should be assisted in putting together a box containing the following, so that you can be independent of the teacher. The list is not exhaustive.

- Scissors
- Rulers
- Pencils
- Colouring pens
- Number lines
- Hundred squares
- Compasses
- Number fans
- Digit cards
- Various types of paper
- Glue sticks
- Dice
- Calculators
- Post-it notes
- Simple maths games, dominoes etc.

One problem sometimes encountered by TAs is that they tend also to be midday assistants and have no time for immediate feedback to the teacher at the end of a lesson immediately prior to lunch. Post-it notes are an excellent resource; they can be helpful in jotting down any necessary comment at any stage of the lesson and can be placed on the wall above the teacher's desk.

Finally, you should have at your disposal several activities or games that you can use with a group if, for example, the group have finished the tasks set. Plenty of these are available, but remember games from your own youth may well be highly appropriate such as 'fizz buzz' and 'I'm thinking of a number'. Ask the teacher, share with colleagues. Many of the published schemes now produce booklets of ideas. Use the Internet, for instance Essex has a web site (www.E-gfl.org). Look for the oral and mental starters section.

10 Supporting ICT and practical subjects

Supporting ICT

Some of the NOS relating to ICT relates to the general principles of supporting pupils and teachers as outlined in the previous chapters, and safety measures as described in the health and safety sections, plus some of the items mentioned in the next section on supporting practical activities. For instance, you will need to provide equipment and resources required by the teacher; know the sort of equipment and resources that are available and their location; the school procedures that must be followed in its use and maintenance; and the reporting of faults or problems. Helping the pupils means maintaining interest, independence and self-confidence in pupils. But there are clearly some specific items relating to ICT that must be considered. Firstly, note that ICT does not just refer to the use of computers and the use of hardware and software, but also, as the scope of the NOS makes clear, overhead projection equipment (OHPs), and recording and playback equipment such as tape and video recorders, and equipment associated with computers and recorders: disks, tape, paper, modems, printers and possibly the video and digital cameras that are in use in many schools.

Electrical safety and security

One of the things all the above have in common is the need for electrical power in the form of connection to the mains or the use of batteries. Both of these have safety risks which must be understood in their use and particularly in the supervision of pupils using the equipment. A very useful couple of pages can be found in *Be Safe* (ASE 2001: 22, 23) or a full account of dealing with electrical matters safely can be found in the Electricity chapter of the secondary safety handbook, *Safeguards in the School Laboratory* (ASE 1996: 57–64), which should be found in every school. Mains electricity must always be treated with care and you should be constantly alert and regularly check for faulty switches, broken sockets or plugs, frayed flexes and any defects in apparatus which could lead to problems [3-17.2:6]. They should never be used. You should label them as dangerous, take them out of use and report their existence immediately, so an early item will be for you to find to whom to report such problems

[3-17.1:6, 7 & iv; 2:xi]. Pupils should be trained from the onset of their contact with any of the above apparatus in its proper use, and the ways of dealing with sockets, switches and connections according to the policy of the school. Some primary schools, for instance, will not allow any pupils to connect or disconnect anything to the mains, others teach the older pupils about switching off first before disconnecting and are happy for pupils to do this. Pupils should be taught from an early age that water and electricity are dangerous together, so wet hands or floors are to be avoided when dealing with any of this equipment. Make sure you know where the nearest fire extinguisher for use with electrical equipment is, and where master switches are in cases of accidents. **Always switch off the power,** if necessary at the mains or the meter, before dealing with any incident or breakdown. If there is an electrical incident, send for help. If you have to act without turning off the power, insulate yourself by standing on a pile of dry paper and use a wooden pole or chair to get the victim away from the source of power.

Batteries need replacing or recharging and may contain toxic materials. Recharging should be done with care, and dud batteries disposed of where indicated by any school procedures. Bulbs are made of fragile glass, a possible hazard in itself. Appropriate storage is important both for the equipment and things like batteries, film, tape and bulbs [3-17.2:9, xii & xiii]. It needs to be safe *and* secure as most of the items mentioned are expensive and sought after.

All items will have come into school with a handbook for their safe and proper use. Find the location of those associated with the equipment you are to use and make yourself familiar with them [3-17.1:3]. Much of the equipment you may already have at home and be familiar with its use, except perhaps for the OHP. It is still worth checking that the school equipment is similar. Switches may be in different places or the sequence of operation different. Always use the appropriate consumables [3-17.2:7]. Cheap tape or paper for some machines can be damaging. Follow the setting up and operating instructions indicated for the machine you are using; again some actions can damage equipment. For instance, OHPs should not be moved until the bulb cools down, as doing so will certainly shorten the life of the bulb but can even cause it to explode. This is particularly true of PowerPoint projectors where a certain routine for switching off is essential to prevent damage.

In order to minimise risks, also be alert for things like the use of the correct furniture [3-17.1:4]. Use of low chairs for computers can cause eye or back strain for the user, trailing flexes through furniture can be hazards. The flexes of OHPs are often encased in rubber treads where they go across the floor to prevent people tripping; computers, screens and printers should be near the power source. You may need to talk to the teacher in charge of the ICT lesson or the ICT coordinator politely if you have a concern [3-17.2:x].

Preparing yourself

Before you work with pupils using ICT equipment, there are several things to do. Check your job description to see what is expected of you and make sure you have any copies of policies or procedures for dealing with ICT equipment [3-17.2:i]. Somewhere there will be instructions as to the storage and maintenance, the use of various sorts of equipment by pupils (or not), who has access and when, how equipment or consumables are allocated and what requirements the school has of anybody using the equipment [3-17.1:i, ii & iii; 2:xii & xiii]. There may be signing out procedures for tape recorders, for instance, or a booking procedure for the video camera. The policy also should have some kind of references to the legislation of which users should be aware, and how the school deals with such matters. For instance, software CDs are often used under licence; you should never use your own disks from home, unless they are approved by the school. The same copyright procedures used for photocopying may be indicated for scanning and printing materials using a computer. The Data Protection Act covers any use of data for compiling databases, say in a class survey. While most schools will operate a firewall preventing inappropriate incoming data getting to the pupils from the Internet, there may be the possibility of child protection issues when pupils start communicating with each other or with other schools. Ensure you understand the school policies and procedures for dealing with virus control and any kind of Internet or email access, use of passwords or other possible sources of problems [3-17.2:ii & iii].

You will need to spend a little study time in self-tuition in the use of any equipment with which you are not familiar, and if you are supporting ICT in the secondary school you may need to undertake further study at a local college to be able to support the secondary curriculum requirements. While pupils with SEN in secondary schools with developmental problems may be operating at levels more usually found in primary schools, and one of the requirements of the secondary curriculum is increasing independence, some of the sophisticated uses of data logging, spreadsheets, email, creating web sites, videoconferencing, even film-making may need you to understand such techniques.

You may need to familiarise yourself with programmes used by the school. If you do not have a computer at home, ask if you can borrow one for a limited time, or use the school machines for practice. Remember there may be a problem with insurance as such equipment is valuable and portable. Do check. If you are not familiar with fax machines, using the Internet or sending emails, do see if there are ways of practising. Try out equipment like tape or video recorders before you use them; nothing is more embarrassing than being given a task to do that the pupils will be really keen to do and then finding something does not work, or a battery is flat, or you have run out of film [3-17.2:v].

Another area of self-study that may be useful is to refer to a copy of the NC for the age group you are working with. Look at the programme of study for the key stage, and at the attainment targets at the end of the NC book (DfEE/QCA 1999a; DfEE/QCA 1999b). Level 2 should describe the achievement of an average seven-year-old, Level 4 an average 11-year-old, Level 5 an average 13-year-old and Level 6 a GCSE equivalent. There is not much reading involved and it will give you some insight into what to expect when you work with pupils. The school may also have a scheme of work or syllabus which will help you know what will be taught in each year group.

General age/stage-related expectations [3-17.2:vii]

Briefly, the NC indicates that children in Years 1 and 2 will be exploring the use of equipment to become familiar with it. They need to get confident that they can operate machines properly and safely, and start to develop their own ideas [3-17.2:ix]. Key Stage 1 children can gather information about their peers and make graphs, enter and store information, plan work and give instructions to things like 'turtles' using logo, and can use a variety of tools and outputs like art programmes or simple databases with lots of pictures. They can describe what they are doing, talk about it, and relate it to what people do outside school in a shop or the home, share their ideas, and review and present their work in a variety of ways. You can encourage all of this talk.

By Key Stage 2, children can use a wide range of tools and sources and begin to use research skills. They should be questioning the plausibility of the information they get and its quality. They can consider the audience of any work they produce, say if using a camera or recording a playlet or a song. They will be able to create databases, classify, check, interpret and think about the information they use. They can organise a variety of sources like word processing and photographic images for simple desktop publishing, monitor different dimensions in the environment, ask 'what if?' questions of simple spreadsheets by changing values – they can get different patterns and relationships. They should be able to share and exchange ideas, and query different ways of doing things.

By Key Stage 3 they are independent users of much ICT equipment, and should be becoming systematic and selective in its use, able to analyse and reflect on what they are doing. They can use different media for testing or problem solving, and produce good quality presentation fit for their purpose. They will email and format web sites, explore the continually evolving forms of communication and suggest improvements.

Key Stage 4 pupils should have developed a holistic approach to using all the various methods currently available, mixing and matching them, easily ICT literate in the world outside school.

Working with pupils

All the usual things apply when you are going to support pupils working in ICT. You need to check out the teacher's requirements and learning intentions for the pupils [3-17.1:1]. Then check the equipment you are going to use. Then with the pupils ensure they are safe and using safe procedures. On computers you can teach them proper sequences and routines for switching on, setting up, and then saving and closing down [3-17.2:1 & i]. With other apparatus such as tape recorders, again routines that are safe and considerate of other users should be reinforced each time you work with the pupils, so that such activities become second nature. You should give them direct guidance on the proper use of expensive equipment; sometimes pupils have developed careless attitudes to property – someone else will clear up, replace, clean, put away. They need to be trained to do these things as well as the actual task in hand [3-17.1:5; 2:2 & iv].

Pupils should be trying things out for themselves, not just working their way through repetitive, occupying games. You can teach skills on the computer like mouse control, or where to 'click' for certain routines, and how to use the printer [3-17.2:2 & 3]. Safe storage of data, film, tape and other materials associated with ICT equipment can all be part of the training. Look at the teachers' schemes of work and planning and where possible discuss with them the general principles that they are trying to teach so that you can follow their intentions [3-17.2:viii]. Where TAs switch on, prepare software and just feed pupils through its use, printing off any attempt at word processing or allowing pupils just to copy out pre-written, corrected text, they will not learn the potential of anything except how to exploit a TA.

As with all school learning, the aim is to get the pupils to think for themselves and act independently of you [3-17.2:4]. You can help in ICT by asking questions like 'Why did you do that?' or 'Why do you think that happened?' or 'What happens if you do . . . ?' One of the problems encountered when Key Stage 2 children begin to search for topic information is their reading ability is not up to the task [3-17.2:vi]. They find some of the search engines obscure in their logic; they will ask a question of a programme but the programme can only answer questions put in a certain style; or they find a page of information and just print it off without any critical appreciation of the contents, as it takes too long for them to read it on screen and select the bit relevant to their needs. You can help them here by ensuring they know what they are supposed to be looking for before they begin – or are they just exploring search methods? Some of the material produced for use on the computers is boring or difficult to access, although another problem is the sheer volume of what is available. This is where trying out materials beforehand and knowing the interest of the pupils you work with will help. It is important to discuss any problems you encounter with what seem to you inappropriate materials – either too hard or too easy – with the teacher in any feedback. You will automatically be monitoring the pupils' successes and problems as they work, and feedback can be as in any other lesson [3-17.1:2 & 6; 2:5]. Do ensure you also report back any problems with the equipment itself.

Finally, try to organise the time you are working with the pupils so that they print off and save work, shut down computers and put away other equipment, rather than you doing it later. It will be your responsibility to make sure all is left safe and secure at the end of any session [3-17.2:8].

Supporting practical subjects

General principles

The general principles of supporting any curriculum subject applies to practical work, but with the added component of making sure you are aware of the safety measures you and the pupils need to take [2-1.1:vi & vii; 3-10.1]. Usually pupils enjoy any kind of practical work, whether it means using tools or media, or working with their own bodies as in PE or drama. However, some pupils, particularly as they get older, become very self-conscious about expressing themselves, or being slower or less competent than others, things like dexterity or clumsiness being more obvious in such subjects. It is important therefore to maintain the fun element of such activities, to be alert for the possibilities of low self-confidence or poor self-esteem in such areas. Many of the skills you may use or techniques you may teach will be of value throughout the pupils' lives, serving as leisure activities or outlets for creativity. Unfortunately, many activities such as performances, matches or field trips have got squeezed out by concerns for safety or completing the more formal, testable parts of the curriculum.

You need to know the learning objectives of the activity you are supporting in just the same way as for any lesson [2-3.1:v]. The activity should have a shape – introduction, the activity itself and review. You will need to plan and prepare, participate, and ensure completion and clearing up by the pupils in your group. Pupils need to discuss their work and that of others constructively, whether it is making sand pies in the reception class or doing a sculpture in the art A level. They need challenge and success. Science, design and technology can all encourage thinking skills and problem solving while using the skills learnt in literacy, numeracy and ICT lessons. Practical subjects will have elements of skills, knowledge and understanding, just as the more formal activities. If you are unsure of any of these, do ask. You should be trained by the teacher in any skills with which you are unfamiliar, and if you are supporting pupils at any higher level, say for external examinations, you may well feel more secure if you actually undertake the qualification for yourself. Have a look at the relevant parts of the NC and any textbooks used by the teacher, not necessarily reading all the words but seeing how diagrams are reproduced for recording, or certain procedures are carried out. You need to know the degree of accuracy for measuring purposes, whether preparing materials, measuring with the pupils or recording. You must familiarise yourself with any tools or apparatus to be used *before* you work with them with the pupils.

Wherever possible, *do not do* the activity for the pupil. Do a separate one and show the pupil how you did it. This goes for cutting out for the youngest pupils to sophisticated science experiments [2-3.2:ii; 3-10.1:4]. Practical skills can only develop by the pupil doing it for themselves. Some of the pupils you support will have physical disabilities which make success in such activities difficult, so your encouragement and praise for small steps of progress are important. Remember the persistence that the paraplegic athletes must have, and the long hours of practice that any successful musician puts in, or your own attempts at learning skills; these kinds of examples will encourage those who easily give up. Pupils with learning problems often achieve success in practical subjects when finding more formal learning daunting.

Case study: An example of practical success

Stephen had struggled to learn the days of the week for all six of his primary school years. He could not recognise the names of them when written down and could not see the purpose of knowing them. His mother told him whether to get ready for school or not. He was a happy boy, satisfied to work with his friend's horses in the school holidays or after school, and popular with his schoolmates in the playground. However, by Year 5 he was pretty fed up with lessons and could not see the purpose of many of them. Then his teacher introduced a DT project which entailed the use of a glue gun. Stephen was dextrous and mastered this tool's use quickly, and completed his model in record time. The teacher then let him show other less dextrous, if more literate pupils how to have success with the glue gun in their DT lessons. School suddenly had a purpose for him.

All the suggestions made for group working, getting pupils organising, planning, talking, questioning, thinking, reviewing and evaluating hold for practical activities. The booklet *Primary Design and Technology – A guide for teacher assistants* (DATA 1996) has some useful tips for showing children how to do something, talking to children while they are working, supporting practical work, supervising a group (including clearing away), organising and maintaining resources and creating a display. The following are some of their tips for helping children in practical work:

- Don't do things for them that they can do for themselves, e.g. *fetch materials, clear away, use tools*
- Encourage them to think about what they are doing and to work carefully
- Remind the children about safe working
- Follow the same rules as the children when using tools or they will soon copy bad habits
- Encourage them to keep their work area tidy, e.g. *return tools and equipment which are no longer needed, put unusable scraps in the bin, rearrange equipment and materials on the table so that it is easier to work*
- Encourage them to be as accurate as possible, e.g. *cutting carefully, measuring food ingredients, marking the position before punching a hole or sticking something down*
- Watch how the children are holding tools and how they have positioned themselves and suggest changes if necessary, e.g. *you might find it easier to stand up to do that, try holding it like this, use this finger to guide it/keep it still*
- Make sure that girls and boys have equal access to tools and equipment – sometimes that is true in theory but not in practice!
- If you need to show a child how to do something, use a spare piece of material rather than their work
- Use the correct names for tools, equipment and materials and help the children to remember them

(p. 19)

Safety

If you are working in a secondary school laboratory, studio, gym or workshop you must ensure that you follow the safety guidelines laid down in the school for staff working in such areas. There are likely to be rules regarding clothing and specialist protective garments, for instance using safety goggles in a laboratory or appropriate shoes in a gym [3-10.1:7]. All staff working in these areas should be trained in the use of any hazardous equipment or when new procedures are introduced [3-10.1:3 & 4]. Do not work in these areas unless you are confident you know what you are doing and can help the pupils you are with to work properly and safely without delay [3-10.1:9]. There are likely to be fewer restrictions in primary schools as the apparatus used and the procedures carried out are less risky. Working in an infant or more particularly a nursery school will mean you are working in a practical way for most of your time, and with young children who are less aware of dangers. ASE's *Be Safe* (2001) and *Safeguards in the School Laboratory* (1996) are excellent booklets and should be available in most schools. One of the things that is pointed out in the latter is that (referring to pupils):

> The biggest danger in the lab is *YOU!* You are a danger whenever you are either *ignorant* or *careless* or both. Remember this because the person most likely to suffer from your mistakes is *YOU!* Report any accident or breakage to your teacher.

It continues with ten rules for behaviour in a secondary laboratory:

1. Only enter a lab when told to do so by a teacher. Never rush about or throw things in the lab. Keep your bench and nearby floor clear, with bags and coats well out of the way.
2. Follow instructions precisely; check bottle labels carefully and keep tops on bottles except when pouring liquids from them; only touch or use equipment and materials when told to do so by a teacher; never remove anything from the lab without permission.
3. Wear eye protection when told to do so and keep it on until all practical work is finished and cleared away.
4. When using a Bunsen burner, make sure that ties, hair etc. are tied back or tucked away.
5. When working with dangerous liquids or heating things, always stand so you can quickly move out of the way if you need to.
6. Never taste anything or put anything in your mouth in the laboratory. If you get something in your mouth spit it out at once and wash your mouth out with lots of water.
7. Always wash your hands carefully after handling chemicals or animal and plant material.
8. If you get burnt or a splash of a chemical on your skin, wash the affected part at once with lots of water.
9. Never put waste solids in the sink. Put them in the bin unless your teacher instructs you otherwise.
10. Wipe up all small spills and report bigger ones to your teacher

(ASE 1996: 25)

You could be working with a group in a cooking activity, or out on the sports field, or using glue guns or craft knives. All of these must be handled safely by you and the pupils you are with. Electrical safety procedures as described in the previous section of this chapter should always be observed. You may be using chemicals that could be dangerous if eaten or handling soil or pond water.

Precautions for doing these activities should be observed, such as covering open cuts with lightweight gloves and ensuring proper hand washing after use. A list of suitable chemicals for primary schools as well as those that are dangerous is included in *Be Safe*, although it is not comprehensive (ASE 2001: 19). The international hazard warning symbols are on page 21 in *Be Safe* and could be displayed and taught to children. It is also the duty of all staff to point out to a more senior member of staff, any hazards noticed in equipment or procedures with which are associated.

It is tempting in these days of increased awareness of danger and risks of litigation, for schools to stop doing many of the interesting and even exciting activities, but this should not happen. Good pupil behaviour is essential when doing practical activities, so you should tell the teacher in charge if you have any concerns about any of the pupils you are working with. Usually, pupils are more interested in 'doing' rather than listening, reading or writing and so often behave better in such lessons, but they can get excited when new activities are introduced. There are many rumours about what is safe practice – or not – that are incorrect. The important thing is that parents should be aware of the nature of activities that will be carried out, the safety precautions that will be taken and the risk assessments that will be carried out, particularly in secondary activities. These will all be spelt out in prospectuses and policies to ensure the school staff are both protected and able to provide an appropriate breadth of experience for pupils.

For instance, it is perfectly possible to heat things in primary science lessons, but some sources of heat are not recommended, such as spirit lamps and picnic stoves. Nightlights, hot water, electric rings, microwave ovens, hair dryers and kilns are all suitable for use in primary schools, but must be used with proper procedures and adult supervision, or only by an adult, e.g. the kiln. You should be taught how to use a Bunsen burner properly in a secondary school if you did not do science recently at school, and understand all the guidelines that go with it, such as using hot wires, test tubes, where and how to put down tapers or matches, and hot items.

Use of glass should be avoided in primary school, but even here accidents can happen and children need to be taught the hazards of glass and what to do if they find something broken. You should know how and where to dispose of broken glass, and where more glass is more widely used as in secondary science lessons, the emergency first aid procedures for dealing with pupils with cuts. Knowing the first aid procedures for dealing with foreign objects or chemicals in eyes when in a laboratory or workshop would also be good practice.

Some lessons include using ourselves or animal parts such as bits of skeletons. Here you must be aware of sensitivities over difference between pupils, e.g. shape, colour or size. Tasting and feeling and smelling things should be done hygienically. Examining soft body parts such as offal is both permissible and safe provided they are fresh and fit for human consumption; eyes of pigs can be used but not those of sheep, cows or goats. You may find pupils dislike this kind of handling, or have cultural or ethical reasons for not taking part. They should never be put under pressure to take part, and the teacher should be told of any problems. Live animals can still be kept in schools but clearly some are more suitable than others, and the proper procedures, safety codes and hygiene facilities should be in place.

Microorganisms such as fungi can be grown in schools but there are proper ways of doing it and of disposing of finished cultures. Yeast growth, yoghurt cultures and examining pond algae are likely to be the extent of work in primary schools, but safe procedures should still be followed. In secondary schools, cultures on special media such as agar will take place and you need to understand the proper ways of dealing with this equipment and its safe disposal. Plants are often grown in schools, both inside and outside in the grounds. Some are hazardous in causing allergies or produce poisonous seeds or leaves.

The school will have comprehensive guidance for taking pupils out of school on visits, whether to static displays in museums, fieldwork or on activity trips. The guidelines must be followed implicitly.

11 Future possibilities – towards the profession of teaching assistance

As I write, the newspapers are full of the announcements of extending the support for teachers in the form of providing more teaching assistants among other things. The proposals are detailed and accompanied by comprehensive consultation documents. It is likely that by the time this book is published, many of the details will be determined, some of the proposed strategies be started and the draft regulations be on their way to becoming statutory. Most teacher unions are supportive of the proposals, but the National Union of Teachers is concerned about the usurping of the teachers' traditional roles by untrained staff. It is important that TAs recognise their limitations and that schools – managers and teachers – do not ask of people more than they are qualified or experienced to do. The new regulations introduce the concept of compulsory supervision for all support staff, to be written into the job description both of the support and supervisory staff who would be qualified teachers. The school management would determine the levels of supervision and its nature using their professional judgement. This means it will be much clearer what TAs with differing qualifications and job descriptions can or should not do, the size of groups they can work with, the nature of their tasks and responsibilities.

You may be reading this book as part of a course and already en route for completing a qualification at Level 2. Some of the possibilities within this level are discussed in the section on Qualifications p. 138. Hopefully, your school will have appointed a mentor or line manager for you when you took up post and you will be able to review your job prospects and competence with an appraiser. You will then need to decide what route you wish to take. You need to discuss these implications with your family, your mentor and line manager. You may not go beyond this Level 2, and be quite happy as a competent TA, but you still need contact with others in your profession to ensure you are continually updating your knowledge and skills. In some job descriptions, your responsibility for continuing professional development is built in. Whether or not it is, you need to always be aware of gaining more knowledge, understanding and skills. Education does not stand still, there is always more to learn and we all are lifelong learners. By undertaking reading about your job, attending meetings or courses of whatever nature, you are enlarging your own horizons and providing a role model for the pupils you work with. While registration and compulsory qualifications for all TAs are not part of the above proposals, if you hope to continue working in a school for any length of time in your present capacity, you would be well advised to consider an accredited qualification of some kind.

Progression

The way is set for a recognised profession of teaching assistance, with various levels of responsibility. The NOS, which this book underpins, are already produced in the two levels which correspond to a competent and an advanced TA – Levels 2 and 3. The proposals (DfES 2002a; DfES 2002b) indicate the definition of 'high-level' teaching assistants with standards to be defined by the Teacher Training Agency (TTA) and that there will be increased funding for recruitment. Some TAs have already got qualifications at a Level 4 – that of undergraduate study – and more are now set on the course of foundation degrees in teaching assistance. These are equivalent to two-thirds of a normal degree.

Only between 10 per cent and 20 per cent of TAs actually want to go on to be teachers; most just want to be good TAs – at whatever level they feel comfortable with. To be a teacher entails having a full degree with QTS, or an NC subject or early years degree and a PGCE. A few people are able to undertake study towards QTS from the two-thirds degree status while still working; currently there is funding for 100 people a year to train 'on the job' for a reduced salary through the Registered Teacher route, but this is also likely to change under the proposals. If you are interested in this route, then do talk to a senior manager in your school or the LEA. Foundation degrees for TAs are not available in all teacher training colleges or universities so you will have to make enquiries as to what is available locally for you. The proposals indicate that there will be 'additional targeted funding over the next three years to develop new training provision and support its local delivery' (DfES 2002a: 8).

Some indication of the kinds of levels of responsibilities that might be expected of the Level 3 and 'high-level' TA are summarised in Table 11.1.

The proposals do not cover any suggestions for making a national agreement over pay and conditions. These are determined locally, but:

> The Government recognises that the proposals . . . may have implications for the pay and conditions of some support staff . . . The National Joint Council for Local Government Services (NJC) which represents the local government employers' organisation and support staff unions, is currently considering the links between duties, skills, competencies and grading for support staff . . . We propose to liaise with the NJC as it develops guidance for schools and LEAs on the framework for grading staff.
>
> (DfES 2002a: 42)

Table 11.1 Possible levels of expectations and competencies for TAs

Level	Competencies expected (Supporting the teacher(s) and personal development)	Experiences typical in school (Supporting the school)	Knowledge and understanding (Supporting the pupil and the curriculum, teaching and learning)	Possible title	Pay scale
1	Carry out instructions; show common sense; follow school policies; relate appropriately to pupils and adults	Domestic chores; basic child care; in class: follow and repeat instructions of teacher	Understands how the school community works and how to be part of a team; takes responsibility for own actions; uses equipment safely	Welfare/care assistant	Entry levels on single status scale
2	Able to work under the direction of teacher, with selected children; assist in classroom task set by teacher; take charge of their own professional development	Facilitate curriculum delivery; carry out practical tasks; work and interact with groups, in sight of teacher; aware of resource provision; see individuals are different; facilitate independence	Has a framework of understanding of learning theory and child development; requires intended learning objectives with activities; supports pupils with SEN and facilitates their learning; attends IEP reviews; carries out NLNS responsibilities after training	Competent teaching assistant	?
3	Able to use initiative appropriately for tasks, especially in private nursery situations, but not take responsibility for children's learning in school; evaluate routines, provide welfare, guidance and support to children	Under direction of teacher: devise resources and activities to support learning; take groups outside classroom; participate in planning and assessment; provide reports and records; perform teaching activities; understand education system and Code of Practice	To have an awareness of parts of the NC, e.g. literacy and numeracy or Early Learning Goals; know about physical, emotional, intellectual, spiritual, cultural development; support children with particular needs and develop expertise; contribute to IEP reviews; relate to parents	Advanced or specialist teaching assistant	?

4	Work in partnership with teachers; share in planning and assessment; contribute to decision making; training and management responsibilities; teaching skills of: exposition, questioning, challenge and behaviour management; working with parents and carers	Can take responsibility, under direction of teacher, for a particular aspect of curriculum development, resource management, or equipment maintenance; able to lead a team of other TAs/adults; take a class using planning directed by teacher and reporting back to teacher. Specialist skills e.g. languages, music, ICT or science technology, phase specialism or SEN area	Able to undertake study with reflection and assignments; understand some of the requirements of the NC; know about learning objectives and aspects of NC; have some understanding of teaching and learning theory; understanding of principles of pedagogy, child development and behaviour management; able to contribute to the formulation of IEPs	Lead or principal teaching assistant — ?
QTS	Undertake responsibility for teaching and learning of pupils; manage additional adults etc.		Teacher requirements	Qualified teacher — Teachers' pay scales

137

Qualifications

As well as the brief references to existing qualifications in the proposals, there is a useful booklet produced by the Employers Organisation (EO) outlining the qualifications for teaching assistants (EO 2002). It describes the national qualifications framework, how NVQs fit into the framework and lists the qualifications that have been accredited by the Qualifications and Curriculum Authority, matching them against the NOS. The list quoted below in Table 11.2 was of those qualifications known by the EO in August 2002. There will be other awarding bodies also submitting their courses for such accreditation. Look at what your local college is providing from this list. NVQs are meant to be assessed by work-based assessors, who check your competencies and question you about your underpinning knowledge. College courses will support this process if they are NVQ-based, or you may prefer a more conventional college course with assignments or even examinations. Whatever course you undertake, there will be an element of workplace-based study and competence assessment. The awarding bodies produce detailed information about their courses, which can sometimes be downloaded from their web sites, requested by telephone or sometimes has to be purchased. It is worth looking at the materials before you undertake a course, just to see what you are letting yourself in for.

Table 11.2 Teaching assistant qualifications accredited to the national qualifications framework in August 2002

Level	Vocationally related qualifications	Occupational qualifications
2	CACHE Level 2 certificate for teaching assistants NCFE Level 2 certificate for teaching assistants Edexcel BTEC certificate for teaching assistants *ABC Level 2 certificate for teaching assistants (under development)* *NOCN Level 2 intermediate award for teaching assistants (under development)*	NVQ Level 2 for teaching assistants (awards by CACHE, OCR, City and Guilds, *Edexcel expected September 2002*)
3	CACHE Level 3 certificate for teaching assistants *Edexcel BTEC Level 3 certificate for teaching assistants (submitted)*	NVQ Level 3 for teaching assistants (awarded by CACHE, OCR, City and Guilds, *Edexcel expected September 2002*)

Items in italics were qualifications submitted but which had not received accreditation when the document was published.
ABC: Awarding Body Consortium
BTEC: Business and Technology Education Council
CACHE: Council for Awards in Children's Care and Education
NCFE: Northern College of Further Education
NOCN: National Open College Network
OCR: Oxford and Cambridge and RSA Examinations
RSA: Royal Society of Arts

© Source: EO 2002: 7

The EO document also gives advice for those of you who may already have some kind of qualification, giving lists of some of the currently accredited qualifications and some not, and spells out the current progression routes to higher education and QTS. It gives the names and contacting details for all the major awarding bodies.

Being a professional

It is now clear that TAs are an accepted part of school life and are found in all schools. They are no longer the hidden staff or invisible, they are highly valued and recognised nationally. The names still vary, and the details of the role are defined by the job description, but their general role of helping the teaching and learning of pupils is understood by the wider public. To be a professional means taking responsibility for that role, and 'performing' to the best of one's ability. Many think of 'the professions' as limited to the law, medicine and the church, sometimes adding in teachers, but the word 'professional' is much wider and indicates a commitment to a code of ethics and practice that is generally recognised. With the NOS publication and the public recognition of the role, TAs must consider themselves professionals. Professionalism is defined in the dictionary as a state indicating quality, character method or conduct, gaining a livelihood and not being an amateur. You do not have a national association yet, your rates of pay do not reflect your role, especially at the higher levels, and union support can only be gained by joining other associations such as Unison or a teacher union. If you want the rights and recognition given to other professions you must consider some responsibilities beyond just turning up for work to carry out your job description. Small local associations are being formed, often as part of other consortium or cluster arrangements, and some more regional associations are beginning to spring up. Hopefully, these will soon form a National Association of Teaching Assistants, able to voice opinions and use their expertise to participate in debates about any future developments.

You are part of a movement to enhance the teaching and learning of pupils, the adults of the future. Your skills and attitudes matter. I wish you continued success in your career, whichever way it takes.

Appendix: Values and Principles Underpinning the National Occupational Standards for Teaching/Classroom Assistants

The National Occupational Standards for teaching/classroom assistants are built upon the following set of agreed values and principles of good practice.

Working in partnership with the teacher

It is the teacher whose curriculum and lesson planning and day-to-day direction set the framework within which teaching/classroom assistants work. The teaching/classroom assistant works under the direction of the teacher, whether in the whole class or on their own with an individual or a small group of pupils. Teaching/classroom assistants, therefore, need to be fully briefed about the teacher's plans and intentions for teaching and learning and her/his contribution to these. Ideally, teaching/classroom assistants will be involved by teachers in their planning and preparation of the work.

Working within statutory and organisational frameworks

Teaching/classroom assistants are an integral part of the school staff team and as such have a responsibility for working to agreed school policies and procedures. In turn, the day-to-day work of the school takes place within a wider legislative framework affecting the content and delivery of the curriculum, health and safety, child protection and other aspects of school life. Teaching/ classroom assistants need to be aware of these school and statutory frameworks, particularly those that directly impact on their own work with pupils.

Supporting inclusion

The principles underpinning inclusive education are those of setting suitable learning challenges, responding to pupils' diverse learning needs, and overcoming potential barriers to learning. Many teaching/classroom assistants are employed with specific responsibilities to work with individual pupils, others are given more general classroom responsibilities. Both roles are key to supporting inclusion by facilitating participation and learning, helping to build confidence, self-esteem and independence so that all pupils are enabled to reach their full potential alongside their peers.

Equality of opportunity

Teaching/classroom assistants have an important role in ensuring pupils' equal access to opportunities to learn and develop. Some pupils need additional or different support in order to have equality of opportunity and teaching/classroom assistants are often employed to provide this for individuals or small groups of pupils. Sometimes, working under the direction of the teacher, teaching/classroom assistants will work with the whole class in order to free up the teacher to work with individual pupils who need special attention.

Anti-discrimination

Teaching/classroom assistants must not discriminate against any individual or group on the grounds of gender, racial origins, religion, cultural or social background, disability or sexual orientation. They must comply with legislation and school policies relating to discrimination and should practise and promote anti-discriminatory practices in all interactions with pupils and colleagues.

Celebrating diversity

Teaching/classroom assistants should demonstrate their valuing of pupils' racial and other personal characteristics in order to help them develop self-esteem and a sense of identity, as well as promoting an understanding and appreciation of different belief systems and cultures in all pupils.

Promoting independence

In providing support for individuals or groups of pupils, teaching/classroom assistants will encourage independence by helping them to develop self-esteem, self-reliance and learning skills as well as increase their subject-related knowledge, understanding and skills. Pupils should be given opportunities to make their own decisions and take responsibility for their own actions.

Confidentiality

Teaching/classroom assistants must adhere to the school policy for the confidentiality of information at all times. This requirement covers information about pupils and colleagues and extends to communications with others in social as well as work-related situations.

Continuing professional development

Teaching/classroom assistants will take advantage of planned and incidental self-development opportunities in order to maintain and improve the contribution that they can make to raising pupil achievement. Asking for advice and support to help resolve problems should be seen as a form of strength and professionalism.

Teaching/Classroom Assistants National Occupational Standards: April 2001
© Copyright Local Government National Training Organisation, 2001

References

Aplin, R. (1998) *Assisting Numeracy*. London: BEAM (The National Numeracy Project and the London Borough of Tower Hamlets).

ASE (1996) *Safeguards in the School Laboratory* (10th edn). Hatfield: Association for Science Education.

ASE (2001) *Be Safe: Health and safety in primary school science and technology* (3rd edn). Hatfield: Association for Science Education.

Balshaw, M. (1999) *Help in the Classroom* (2nd edn). London: David Fulton Publishers.

DATA (1996) *Primary Design and Technology: A guide for teacher assistants*. Wellesbourne: Design and Technology Association.

DfEE (1996) 'Supporting pupils with medical needs in schools' (Circular 14/96). London: Department for Education and Employment.

DfEE (1998a) 'Excellence for all children: meeting special educational needs' (Green Paper). London: Department for Education and Employment.

DfEE (1998b) *Meeting Special Educational Needs: A programme of action* (MSENPAS). London: Department for Education and Employment.

DfEE (1998c) *The National Literacy Strategy* [Guidance: Framework for Teaching]. London: Department for Education and Employment.

DfEE/QCA (1999a) *The National Curriculum: Handbook for primary teachers in England: Key Stages 1 and 2*. London: Department for Education and Employment and Qualifications and Curriculum Authority.

DfEE/QCA (1999b) *The National Curriculum: Handbook for secondary teachers in England: Key Stages 3 and 4*. London: Department for Education and Employment and Qualifications and Curriculum Authority.

DfEE (1999c) *The National Numeracy Strategy* [Framework for teaching mathematics]. London: Department for Education and Employment.

DfEE (1999d) *National Literacy Strategy: Additional Literacy Support (ALS)* [Teaching materials]. London: Department for Education and Employment.

DfEE (1999e) *The National Literacy Strategy: Phonics. Progression in phonics: materials for whole class teaching*. London: Department for Education and Employment, Standards and Effectiveness Unit.

DfEE (1999f) *The National Literacy Strategy: Spelling Bank*. London: Department for Education and Employment.

DfEE (1999g) *The National Numeracy Strategy: Mathematical vocabulary book*. London: Department for Education and Employment, Standards and Effectiveness Unit.

DfEE (2000a) *Working with Teaching Assistants: A good practice guide*. London: Department for Education and Employment.

DfEE (2000b) *Teaching Assistant File: Induction training for teaching assistants*. London: Department for Education and Employment.

DfEE (2000c) *Behaviour Management Module – Induction training for teaching assistants*. London: Department for Education and Employment.

DfEE (2000d) *Handbook for Leading Mathematics Teachers*. London: Department for Education and Employment.

DfES (2001a) *Special Educational Needs Code of Practice*. London: Department for Education and Skills.

DfES (2001b) *Teaching Assistant File – Induction training for teaching assistants in secondary schools*. London: Department for Education and Skills.

DfES (2001c) *The National Literacy Strategy – Developing Early Writing*. London: Department for Education and Skills.

DfES (2002a) *Developing the Role of School Support Staff* (Consultation DfES/0751/2002). London: Department for Education and Skills.

DfES (2002b) *Time for Standards* (Proposals DfES/0751/2002). London: Department for Education and Skills.

DOH, HO and DfEE (1999) *Working Together to Safeguard Children*. London: The Stationery Office, Department of Health, Home Office, Department for Education and Employment.

EO (2002) *Qualifications for Teaching Assistants* (Guidance Version 1). London: Employers Organisation.

Fox, G. (1998) *A Handbook for Learning Support Assistants*. London: David Fulton Publishers.

Fox, G. (2001) *Supporting Children with Behaviour Difficulties*. London: David Fulton Publishers.

Fox, G. and Halliwell, M. (2000) *Supporting Literacy and Numeracy – A guide for learning support assistants*. London: David Fulton Publishers.

Freeman, R. and Meed, J. (1993) *How to Study Effectively*. London: National Extension College and Collins Educational Ltd.

Freiberg, H. J. and Stein, T. A. (1999) 'Measuring, improving and sustaining healthy schools'. In H. J. Freiberg (ed.) *School Climate*. London and Philadelphia: Falmer Press.

Hook, P. and Vass, A. (2000) *Confident Classroom Leadership*. London: David Fulton Publishers.

LGNTO (2001) *Teaching/Classroom Assistants National Occupational Standards*. London: Local Government National Training Organisation.

Northledge, A. (1990) *The Good Study Guide*. Milton Keynes: The Open University.

Ofsted (1999) *Handbook for Inspecting Primary and Nursery Schools*. London: Ofsted.

Ofsted (2002) *The Curriculum in Successful Primary Schools* (HMI 553). London: Ofsted.

QCA (1999a) *The National Numeracy Strategy – Teaching mental calculation strategies: guidance for teachers at Key Stages 1 and 2* (QCA/99/380). London: Qualifications and Curriculum Authority.

QCA (1999b) *The National Numeracy Strategy – Teaching written calculations: guidance for teachers at Key Stages 1 and 2* (QCA/99/486). London: Qualifications and Curriculum Authority.

144

Rogers, B. (1991) *'You Know the Fair Rule'*. Harlow: Longman.

Rogers, B. (1994) *Behaviour Recovery*. Harlow: Longmans.

Schonveld, A. (1995) *Schools and Child Protection*. Coventry: Community Education Development Centre.

Watkinson, A. (2002) *Assisting Learning and Supporting Teaching*. London: David Fulton Publishers.

Index